The
Bhagavad Gita

Goswami Kriyananda

The Temple of Kriya Yoga

Other books by Goswami Kriyananda

The Spiritual Science of Kriya Yoga
The Wisdom and Way of Astrology (new edition)
Inner Teachings on the Laws of Karma
Beginner's Guide to Meditation
Intermediate Guide to Meditation
Letters from the Guru-Methodology of Kriya Yoga
Kriya Yoga Sutras with Commentary
The Moon: The Most Vital Planet in Your Chart
Karmic Astrology: Retrograde Planets and Past Lives
The Sun of God
Extraordinary Spiritual Potential
The Kriya Yoga Upanishad and the Mystical Yoga Upanishads
Pathway to God-Consciousness
How to Have a Vision
Guru/Disciple Relationship
Predict Your Future
The Chakras: Mass-Energy Converters (Stepping Stones to Enlightenment)
Comparative Astrology
Beginner's Guide to Astrology
La science spirituelle du Kriya Yoga
Guide pratique de meditation
Su Primer Guiá de Meditación
La scienza spirituale dello yoga di Kriya

Booklets

The Kriya Yoga Sutras
Blue Lotus Sutra
Kriya Bindu
Dharma Bindu
Isha Upanishad
Upanishad Series I
Upanishad Series II
Hong Sau Upanishad
Physiology for Mystics
Key Concepts in Hindu Thought

Other Temple Publications

Yoga, You, Your New Life by Swami Japananda

The Bhagavad Gita

Goswami Kriyananda

The Temple of Kriya Yoga

Dedicated to: Mata Sita—the first to hear—Sandy Jette and Karen Phillips. May they awaken in peace.

Foreword

The Gita is based upon a clearly defined cosmology, the
central principle being the 'Reality without attributes',
which can be realized through Samadhi. The nature of this
Reality is Existence, Wisdom and Bliss. Arjuna's chosen
symbol of the Reality, Ishvara, is personified as Lord
Krishna, the perfect expression of compassion and truth.

The Reality external is Brahman, the Reality indwelling is
Atma. Atma is Brahman, just as the wave is the ocean, or
the drop of water is the lake.

Samadhi, or balanced self-conscious awareness, is the
realization of the unity of Atma and Brahman. The
pathways and methods of attaining Samadhi comprise the
essence of the Gita. When a soul is freed from attachment
to objects and the fruits of labor through yogic discipline,
consciousness is then capable of Samadhi.

Sri Sri Brahman manifests in three modes: as Lord
Brahma, Lord Vishnu, and Lord Shiva. Brahma is the
principle of projection, Vishnu of preservation, and
Shiva of transformation. The universe, as the mani-
festation of these three modalities, is neither created nor
destroyed; it is, rather, projected from Unmanifest
Reality, as a dream is projected from the sleeping mind,
dissolving again upon awakening. The universe is
beginningless and endless, a process of rotation, a dance
of phases, the dream of the Great God. The projection of
the universe is called the Day of Brahma, and its
dissolution is Brahma's Night.

The universe is a duality of Matter and Spirit, both
eternal and ever-interacting. Matter has three modes and
acts through them, creating the cycles of time and space
in a spiraling evolution to superconscious awareness and
freedom.

ARJUNA!
SYMBOL OF
IDEAL DEVOTEE,
PERFECT
DISCIPLE.

The Bhagavad Gita, the Song of God, is a spiritual
dialogue between Sri Krishna (Ishvara, the Divinity) and
Arjuna, a soul seeking the answers to the eternal
dilemmas of the earthly life. Their discourse takes place
on Kurukshtra, the field of the heart's desire. The soul,
as it attempts to merge its life with Life, to dream its
dream in harmony with the universe, is poignantly
portrayed upon these pages.

There are four main speakers in the Gita: Arjuna, Sri
Krishna, the Blind King, and Sanjaya.

The Blind King hears the dialogue between Sri Krishna
and Arjuna through his clairvoyant and clairaudient
advisor, Sanjaya. The king's one hundred sons (the
Kauravas) are challenging Arjuna and his brothers (the
Pandavas) to battle. The battle is allegorical, not
historical. The 'field' is the soul, and the action, the
characters and the dialogue transcend culture, place and
time. The king is spiritually blind, although his
generative power is enormous. He has one hundred sons
who are greedy, ruthless and ambitious. They are
prepared to do battle with the five Pandavas, the five
balanced chakras, led by Arjuna whose name means the
Whiteness of the Shining Intellect. Sri Krishna, the Sun
Center, is the advisor and charioteer of Arjuna.

The Gita answers the perennial questions, bringing
soothing balm to the world-weary heart, uplifting the
soul and offering the spiritual keys which unlock the
doorway to the wisdom of harmonious living. The Gita is
a revelation of the royal road of universal unselfish love.

May those keys be given unto you, who read and meditate
upon these teachings, and especially to you who share
these teachings with others. May your heart's desire and
longing merge with the dream of the Great Spirit, whose
essence is the essence of all beings.

Table of Contents

MAHABHRATA
↳ INDIA'S GREAT
EPIC POEM
OF WHICH THE
B. GITA IS APART OF.

The Battle Within

SPIRITUAL BATTLE BETWEEN PSYCHOLOGICAL FORCES OF MATERIAL IGNORANCE + FORCES OF HIGHER DISCRIMINATIVE MIND + SOUL

1

"MANAS," SENSE-CONSCIOUS MIND

DHRITARASHTRA

The Blind King asked:
AKA THE BLIND MIND

KURUKSHETRA WAR

KURUS WICKED IMPULSIVE MENTAL + SENSE TENDENCIES

1 On the field of duty, on the field of desire,
   Assembled ready to resolve who is final sire,
   — My hundred sons and the five sons of Pandu —
   What did they do, what did they do?

PANDAVAS DISCRIMINATIVE TENDENCIES

"DIVINE INSIGHT" INTROSPECTIVE

Sanjaya answered:

MATERIAL DESIRE

2 Oh King, your son Duryodhana, seeing the Pandu,
   Determined never for peace to sue,
   Went then to his teacher Drona to see
   The mighty force of their great army.

"BUDDHI," DISCRIMINATIVE INTELLIGENCE

SAMSKARAS, INNER TENDENCY, HABIT

3 Duryodhana said: Behold the host of Pandu's force
   By Drupada's son arrayed in military mold.
   He is your pupil drawing from your mind's source
   His loyalty to you he has not sold.

4 Here are the heroes of old:
   Strength and Mind we are told,
   Warriors like Success and Protection too,
   Even the Greatness of the Vehicle True.

PANDUS

5 There are also powerful warriors
   Like Prosperity and Calmness,
   Purity and Double Victory then,
   And Valor, bull among men.

THE KLEASAS

6   There is Mighty Courage and Powerful Glory,
     The Son of Honor and the Five Sons of Faith.
     Together they capture their competitors
     For all are great and powerful warriors.

7   And our own distinguished men, power-born,
     Taught by you and the best of the twice-born.
     Who are these leaders of our host
     Qualified to lead my army foremost?

8   They include you, Anger and Attachment for sure
     Pity, Death and Cruelty to lure,
     And Falsehood, the son of Sense Enjoyment
     Is always victorious in the battle over the poor.

9   Many other heroes well-equipped for life
     Come prepared to sacrifice for my cause;
     All are experienced in military strife,
     They stand ready, yet paused.

10   Our army's strength is multitudinous
     And perfectly protected by the wise Bhisma,   — EGO
     Whereas the strength of the Pandavas is limited
     And protected only by the unskilled Bhima.

11   So do not your military leader disappoint
     Let each be at his strategic point.
     Guard and protect Bhisma above all
     Each and every one of you be at his call.

12   Then Bhisma, grandsire of the Kuru dynasty,
     Grandfather of the warriors, blew his conch shell;   — "AUM"
     Like a lion's roar it resounded   HOLY VIBRATION
     To the very gates of hell it sounded death's knell.   LINK BETWEEN
                                                            MATTER + SPIRIT

13   Then conch shells and kettledrums
     Followed by cymbals and cow horns
     All suddenly sounded and resounded
     Their combined clamor everywhere abounded.

EGO = LOUD

14   On the other side, the Intellect and the Mind
      Stood in their great chariot drawn by horses white,
      Blew their wondrous conch shells of cosmic insight,
      Signing the enemy's destiny that very night.

ARJUNA IS MEDITATING + EGO IS TERRIFIED.

15   Lord Krishna blew his conch called Meditation,
      Arjuna, winner of Wealth, blew his conch, Devotion;
      And Strength, accomplisher of deeds of non-emotion,
      Blew his conch called austerity-in-motion.

16   King Truth blew his conch, Dharma,
      Patience and Control blew conches Sacrifice and Gift;
      Truth practices Duty while Patience and Control
      Perform the sacrificial rite, the mind to lift.

17   Greatest of archers, the King of Kashi,
      Purity, and the great warrior Humility,
      Along with Contentment and Protection too
      Formed the ranks of the blessed and true.

18   Greatness, the Sons of Faith,
      And the Son of Honor, greatly armed,
      All blew their celestial conches
      And moved into battle form.

19   The combined celestial conches   *CHAKRAS*
      Did so amplify through earth and sky
      That the Blind King's men knew
      It was their time to die.

20   Seeing the Blind King's army poised, ready to strike,
      Arjuna, under the banner of Lord Hanuman,   *PRANAYAMA*
      Raised his holy bow and prepared to defend   *"LORD*
      The honor of his clan and the Truth to mend.   *OF BREATH"*

21   Then, Oh Lord of Earth,
      Arjuna spoke thus to Sri Krishna:
      Oh Master of the Senses, let me the armies see
      By placing my chariot at the proper degree.

22   Allow me to see the men on this field
      Desiring to do battle today,
      Those with whom I must fight
      For this karma to pay.

23   Allow me to see the warriors here,
      Serving the Blind King's ignorant sons,
      Not knowing anyone as their peer,
      Thus assembled, waiting karma to be done.

24   Sanjaya continued: Oh Seed of the Night, [BLIND KING]
      Sri Krishna moved the resplendent chariot car
      Out between the two armies at twilight [BALANCE]
      And halted it afar before the morning star.

25   Now in front of Bhisma and Drona
      And the other leaders of this world
      Sri Krishna said: Arjuna, behold
      How the Kauravas fit the karmic mold. [ACTION, UNCOINSCIOUS]

26   There, in the midst, Arjuna could see
      Fathers, teachers, uncles and sons,
      Grandsons and friends old and yet to be;
      Armies arrayed with weapons by the ton.

27   When Arjuna saw his friends as well
      He was filled with deep compassion
      And overwhelmed with fears of hell.
      Thus he spoke: This ought not be done.

28   Arjuna said: My Krishna dear,
      I am despondent, can you not hear?
      Am I ready to fight friends and family too,
      What is this I am about to do?

29   My limbs fail me
      And my mouth is parched
      My hair stands upright
      At this ungodly sight.

30   My bow is slipping from my hand,
      My skin burning like the hottest sand;
      l cannot find a place to stand
      My mind wanders from this battle land.

31   Krishna, I foresee many omens unkind.
      I cannot see the good in slaying my kind.
      It seems that all has been reversed;
      In this drama have I been cursed?

32   Krishna, I wish not victory
      Nor pleasure nor empire.
      What benefit can be acquired
      By being enmeshed in this karmic desire?

33   Those for whom I seek joy to acquire
      Are poised, ready for the battle's fire,
      Risking life, wealth and empire;
      What would be mine, an empty victory, sire?

34   There are teachers, fathers and sons,
      Also grandfathers and grandsons as well,
      Maternal uncles and fathers-in-law
      And other relatives ready for death's fall.

35   Oh Krishna, I do not wish to slay,
      Though they would kill me this day;   — TRIPLE COSMOS:
      Not for the throne of the three universes   *CAUSAL (MENTAL),
      Much less for earth with its seeming curses.   ASTRAL (ENERGY)
                                                     PHYSICAL (MATTER)

36   Oh Krishna, what happiness can come to me
      From slaying the Blind King's army?
      In slaying these wretched souls, what gain?
      None at all, it can only bring pain.

37   Oh Krishna, our kinsmen we ought not kill
      Though we have the greater warring skill.
      Can we break free from this earth's bind
      By the killing of our own kind?

OUL SEEKING TO ANSWERS TO LIFE.

[ARJUNA] REALIZES THAT HE HAS TO DESTROY HIS MATERIAL TENDENCIES. BECAUSE OF HIS FAMILIRITY W/ THEM, HE FEELS SYMPATHETIC OF THEM.

38   They see not the wrong of their deeds
      For they are blinded by their greed;
      But we know what is to be done, to slay none
      Asat karma comes from killing family seed.

      SAMSKARAS

39   We who clearly see this as wrong
      Should seek to make the family strong.
      Have we not learned to avoid this road
      Thereby overcoming karma's heavy load?

40   When the family unit disintegrates,
      To the laws of life we no longer dedicate.
      When family traditions disappear,
      The entire clan lives in virtueless fear.

41   When disorder prevails, wives become unwise,
      When wives become unwise, culture is tossed aside;
      When culture fails, duty is lost
      And many souls count the cost.

42   When duty is lost, life is pain
      For the destroyer and destroyed.
      Then the sacred rites no longer bind
      The ancestors and their earthly kind.

43   Actions which destroy the family
      Cause the loss of the sacred duty.
      When broken, forgotten are the ancient rites,
      The ancestors lose their astral sight.

44   Oh Krishna, we have been told
      That family souls will be lost,
      Will wander in realms tempest-tossed
      And be ever silent to our thought.

45   Alas, a great wrong, this killing of seed
      That I resolved to commit by karmic deed.
      Am I driven by a royal greed,
      This kingdom-land I do not need.

46 Oh Krishna, it would be better today
If the Blind King's sons were me to slay,
Without resistance, as I here passively lay,
And let these demonic ones have their way.

47 Arjuna sank down in his chariot of gold,
Tossed aside his arrows and his bow,
His mind was troubled and in woe
He said, I will not fight! No, no, no.

The Victorious Sage

2

1   Krishna, seeing Arjuna overwhelmed,
    Despondent, eyes tear-filled to the brim,
    Spoke these words to him:
    My friend, what is this whim?

2   Arjuna, what is this helplessness?
    Why this ignoble faint-heartedness
    At the moment of battling?
    Here stands the enemy, their spears rattling.

3   Arjuna, scorcher of foe,
    Allow not this unmanliness
    To overpower your soul.
    Awake, arise, attain your goal.

4   Krishna, how can I continue in this way?
    I cannot Bhiṣma and Drona slay,   *these* SUMSKANAS
    For they are worthy of spiritual light.
    Why are we enmeshed in this plight?

5   Better a beggar in this world to be
    Than to drown in this catastrophe.
    By killing to gain my just right
    I turn my life into a dark night.

6   I do not know which is the better way
     To carry a curse or to die this day.
     If I slay the sons of the Kuru,
     Could I live with broken taboo?

7   I am overwhelmed with weakness,
     I don't know what to do.
     I am your pupil, I wish not to guess;
     Tell me, oh Lord, which way is best.

8   What is the way to relieve this anxiety?
     Which path is worthy of life's ecstasy?
     I know this anxiety cannot be stilled
     By astral kingdoms or the power of the will.

9   Arjuna turned to the Lord and said:
     Krishna, restorer of the Earth,
     I will not fight,
     Yet know I am not filled with fright.

10   Then Krishna, with a semblance of a smile,
     Standing in the midst of the armies
     Spoke to Arjuna who was faltering:
     Walk on awhile, just another mile.

11   Grieve not for the forms you see.
     Lament not for what ceases to be.
     Wise souls are not anxious about death or life
     In the things of this world they find no strife.

12   Arjuna, I speak to you true:
     I, these noble warriors, and also you
     Were in the past eternally
     And in the future we shall always be.

13   Without destruction of our souls, like the sage,
     We pass from babyhood through youth to old age.
     Then we pass into another body, into a new age.
     The wise are not bewildered by this body's cage.

14 Pleasure and pain come because of loss and gain.
   Their appearance and disappearance in due season
   Spins like the wheel of the seasons;
   Thus fearlessly live finding the reasons.

15 The soul who experiences pleasure and pain,
   Without anxiety, with peace of mind,
   Surely immortality will find,
   Knowing the fullness of the Life Divine.

16 The Seers of old have said again and again:
   What is non-existent cannot come to be;
   What is existent cannot cease to see.
   Thus the Seers of old lived sanely and free.

17 Know this: That which pervades the entire body
   Is, in truth, indestructible, this is the key.
   Can you not see that none can destroy
   Imperishable Spirit, It is not an alloy.

18 These perishable bodies are
   The embodiment of the Imperishable.
   Bodies shall all cease to be;
   Therefore, Arjuna, stand and be free.

19 He who thinks himself a slayer,
   He who thinks himself slain,
   Grasps not the truth that karma we must pay.
   Atma is never slain, nor does It ever slay.

20 Atma was never born, Atma will never die,
   It will never cease to be;
   Unborn, Eternal, existing without nadi,
   Atma ceases not with the death of the body.

21 Who knows as indestructible
   This unborn, eternal and immutable Goal,
   Can never slay or cause a soul to slay.
   Death of the body does not destroy the soul.

YOUR HIGHER SELF
ONLY PURIFIES
THE LOWER SELF,
IT DOES NOT DESTROY IT.

22   As you discard your clothes worn-out,
      You put on fresh ones without a doubt.
      As your body dies, another do you take;
      You will continue to live, for this is fate.

23   Atma, Earth smothers not, it gives material birth.
      Atma, Fire burns not, Fire gives spiritual attire.
      Atma, Water wets not, it gives feelings that were.
      Atma, Air dries not, Air gives intellect rare.

THE SELF

24   This Atma is unbreakable and indissoluble,
      Incombustible and inevaporatable.
      This Atma is ever-existing, all-pervading,
      Unmoved, unmoving and eternally surveying.

25   This Atma is invisible, inconceivable,
      Immutable and unchangeable.
      And knowing Atma to be so
      You need never worry over life's flow.

26   Even if you think of the Atma
      As constantly born, constantly dying,
      Even then you should not lament
      Even then remain content.

27   For whatever takes birth, death is its final curtain,
      And for whatever dies, rebirth is certain.
      Therefore, in the performance of your task,
      Hold to the Dharma, do not the karma grasp.

28   Beings emanate from an unmanifest state
      And manifest at an intermediate date.
      And they go to their fate in the end
      To begin this cycle that begins again.

29   Some behold the soul as thunderous
      Some describe the soul as wondrous
      But know It and be stirred,
      Be the Word.

30 Arjuna, the Spirit in each body is a miracle,
You need not worry or be fearful,
Nor mourn for any sentient creature;
We shall all reach the great Cosmic Teacher.

31 By holding fast to your own Dharma,
You will not tremble at your karma.
A warrior brave should scale the wall;
Arjuna, stand and answer Dharma's call.

32 Happy indeed are the warriors of old
Who find themselves in the battle fold.
To perform one's Dharma, it is said of old
Is to find the celestial planets of gold.

33 Arjuna, if you refuse this Dharma call,
You will fall and forfeit your all.
Reputation will be lost, misfortune found;
Stand! This is your Dharma ground.

34 People forever will speak of your fear
They will recount it over your funeral bier.
To those honored, dishonor is worse than death;
Death of name, death of fame, an unholy shame.

35 Great leaders who hold your name in esteem
Will think you have fled from the battle stream.
The truth of your thoughts they will not gleam
They will think you a coward, or so it will seem.

36 Cruel words about your clan they will say,
For your muddled mind Dharma doth slay.
Look, Arjuna, where you are
For you are unable to see afar.

37 You will die in the performance of your Dharma
And attain the higher astral plane,
Or you will be conqueror enjoying earthly gain.
Therefore, arise and fight through your pain.

38   Become detached from pleasure and pain,
      Wisdom and wealth, loss and gain.
      Gird thyself for the battle true
      In the service of your Krishna Blue.

39   Ultimate wisdom has been explained to you
      Through the knowledge of Sankhya true.
      Now the wisdom of Kriya that you are to pursue
      Will free you from craving, showing you what to do.

40   Freedom from craving relieves frustration.
      Even short practice of detachment brings
      The mastery over worldly things;
      There is advancement untold on this path of gold.

41   Arjuna, the confident mind is joy-filled,
      By walking the path craving is stilled.
      Those of uncertain mind are self-willed,
      Through craving the road is forever uphill.

42   Undiscerning souls say that the Vedas are all
      They do not see or hear the deeper call.
      They say there is nothing else, that this is all;
      Their flowery words are absurd and small.

43   Their souls are ridden with desire,
      And yearning to become earth's sire
      They excite new interests for reward
      For pleasure and power they take up the sword.

44   In souls intent on pleasure and power,
      The mind's too scattered to ascend the tower.
      The scattered mind becomes spiritually sour
      And finds not serenity in the quiet hour.

45   The Vedas deal with the gunas three
      Transcend these modes and become free.
      Rid yourself of gaining and guarding
      Be equipoised: Balance your cosmic tree.

TRIFOLD REINCARNATION-
MAKING QUALITIES OF
HUMAN NATURE:
SATTVIC (ELEVATING)
RAJASIC (ACTIVATING)
TAMASIC (DEGRADING

46   To the one who has attained the Ultimate Song,
     The teachings of the Vedas are like a pond
     That has been covered by a great flood
     Such a being overflows with Holy Love.

47   Arjuna, you have a rightful claim to work
     For work's sake only, not for the fruits of work.
     Desire for the fruits must never be your goal
     Renounce your laziness, arouse your soul.

48   Act with detachment to loss or gain,
     In success or failure, be not stained.
     Equanimity of mind is self-control,
     The mark of a spiritual soul.

49   To strive for reward is contrary indeed
     To the ancient holy yoga creed.
     Follow the course of wisdom true
     Be not miserable: Be Ever-New.

50   Endowed with serenity, shed anxiety,
     Discard the ill-done and the well-done.
     Devote yourself fully to Kriya Yoga
     Enjoy spiritual action on every loka.

51   In embracing serenity, abandoning rewards,
     The wise put aside their earthly swords.
     And freed from the shackles of desire,
     They no longer burn in craving's fire.

52   When your mind transcends the jungle of delusion,
     You will remove attachment's confusion.
     All allurement and aversion are in the mind
     Put them aside, your goal to find.

53   Mind, no longer bewildered by the various ways,
     Becomes unperturbed, remains fixed and free.
     Self-sustained, you gain a way out of the maze,
     And thus you find the samadhi key.

54   Krishna, how can one identify a soul fixed in God?
     How do the Illumined talk? How do they walk?
     How do they sit? How was that peace light lit?
     Can it be understood, this great cosmic good?

55   Arjuna, a soul knowing the bliss of Atma
     Wanting nothing more, never bored,
     Relinquishes all desire for rewards.
     That soul I call illumined, king of lords.

56   That soul who remains unshaken by sorrow,
     Not desiring the pleasures of earth's show
     Is indeed freed from anger, freed from fear
     That soul I call illumined, truly a seer.

57   When that soul is lucky, the heart does not leap
     When unlucky, the Illumined do not overly weep.
     Forever without compulsion, this soul is unconfined
     I call that soul illumined and of stable mind.

58   As the tortoise draws in his limbs,
     The seer continuously draws in his whims;
     For him this earth's lure dims.
     I call that soul illumined, Lord of cherubims.

59   On the day the limbs are first drawn within,
     Sense enticements begin to dim.
     Yet the taste persists, to enter the mind they insist
     Til the mystic vision returns That which pre-exists.

60   Turbulent by nature the senses are
     Pulling the mind from the path circular.
     Return, return to the pilot star,
     The celestial car of the avatar.

61   By recollecting the mind, the soul does thrill.
     In asan still, find the holy domicile.
     With skill that mind does instill My peace;
     That soul is illumined, on the path of release.

62 Dwelling on objects, externally or internally,
    The mind becomes attached eternally.
    Attached, the mind becomes addicted by degree.
    Thwart that addiction and the mind becomes angry.

63 Be angry and the mind is confused by pretense.
    Confuse your mind, forgotten is experience.
    Forget experience and you lose discernment,
    Lose discernment and you miss life's ascent.

64 When a soul has severed hatred and lust,
    That soul walks safely on this earth's crust.
    Senses controlled and under the will,
    That soul is illumined, the mind tranquil.

65 The attainment of the mind's tranquility
    Brings all sorrow to an end eloquently.
    By withdrawing the mind from its shallow surface,
    The sage is held firmly to life's holy purpose.

66 The uncontrolled mind cannot feel
    That the Spirit is real or at the wheel.
    How can such a soul meditate
    Or steer toward that starry gate?

67 As a strong wind can turn a ship from its course,
    Mind is cast adrift by wandering from its source.
    Thus the soul is turned from its better judgment
    When the mind is caught in sense enslavement.

68 Therefore, that soul who understands
    That the senses are not to be fanned
    Will master life by becoming detached;
    That sage is illumined, to God firmly latched.

69 Without meditation can peacefulness abound?
    Without tranquility where is happiness found?
    Without inturning there can only be strife,
    Without happiness what is life?

70   Water continually into life's ocean does flow
      Yet the ocean remains in status quo.
      Desire into the sage's mind does flow
      Yet he fixes on Me and continues to grow.

71   That soul knows peace who has renounced desire,
      Free from longings, his soul sings.
      Living without fear, grief or hell's desire,
      That soul is illumined, attuned to life's choir.

72   Arjuna, this is the Brahmic Bliss state,
      There is no more to elucidate.
      No soul falls back from It to delusion.
      Even in death there is no confusion.

The Yoga of Service

3

1 Krishna, if you consider knowledge
To be superior to action,
Why are you urging me
To this destructive passion?

2 Krishna, you drive me to distraction
For on your words I truly cling.
Tell me definitely one disciplined thing
By which I may attain the Divine Flame.

3 Arjuna, to Illumination there are two ways
Which were taught by Me in the ancient days:
The path of knowledge that leads to the Self
And selfless action bringing spiritual wealth.

4 In action you gain freedom from karma,
In action, attain the perfect Dharma.
By renunciation alone,
You cannot become Om.

5 Surely none can remain inactive for long
For all are driven by karma inborn.
Whether their lives be short or long,
Quickly they learn inaction is wrong.

6   By the outward control of action and sense,
     A soul can still be inwardly violent.
     By outwardly restraining and inwardly remaining
     Unfit, a soul becomes a spiritual hypocrite.

7   When the organs of action and sense are refined
     By the inner power of the disciplined mind,
     The unattached soul can then undertake
     The sacrament of Kriya for its own sake.

                         FOR ME IS NOT PRESENT DURING "ACTION"

8   Perform your allotted duty for Me.
     Inaction is unwise, in action be free.
     By denying action you can't even maintain
     A physical body or a mind sane.

9   A soul is bound by bonds of karma
     When it acts to obtain an end.
     Be free from attachment, do your Dharma
     And the sacrifice will be your friend.

10   The father of creation created mankind
     With his holy sacrifice benign.
     He said: Regenerate through this sacred rite
     And obtain life's bliss through meditative insight.

                    DEITIES
11   Succor unto the devas through this ritual
     And the devas will succor unto you.
     In attuning to each other unattached
     You allow the highest good to be unlatched.

12   Fostered by sacrifice, the Lord will,
     Unasked, bestow on you life's fill.
     Partaking of life's gifts so bestowed
     Without sharing brings on the karma load.

13   Noble souls take what is left after the sacrifice
     And are so saved from the karmic vise.
     Those who cook food for the body only
     Ingest emotions and miss the paradise holy.

14   Beings have evolved from thought-food.
      From rain this food comes in plenitude.
      From sacrifice comes the golden rain in gratitude.
      Sacrifice originates in action, begins in solitude.

15   Action has its origin in scripture,
      These words proceed from the cosmic stir
      The whirling wheel zodiacal;
      Every ritual is the Lord's wisdom-call.

16   He who does not follow this prescribed sacrifice
      Leads a life of foolishness and vice.
      By living only for sensual pleasure
      You will never find the cosmic measure.

17   He who takes delight in the Atma alone,
      Is illumined in That and there has his home.
      Who rejoices only in the Atma's delight,
      Has no prescribed duty, is free in the Light.

18   Great souls have not the need to do
      Nor do they leave things undone.
      They have no selfish dependence
      On any kind of creature experience.

19   By doing your duty with attachment
      Your life will go to extremes;
      By doing your work without attachment
      You will attain the Supreme.

20   It is through perfected action alone
      That wise souls reach the unknown.
      Be ever-mindful of the cosmic balance;
      Act, but in that action, be passionless.

      — ABHYASA + VAIRAGYA

21   Whatever actions great souls do,
      Those things the world takes on anew;
      Whatever standards great souls set,
      The masses these same standards beget.

22   Arjuna, for Me there is nothing to be gained
      In the three worlds or on any plane;
      Nothing unattained, nought to be begun,
      Yet I do not action frown upon.

23   If I did not engage in unwearied action,
      The three universes would enter into contraction. — PHYSICAL
      Yogis follow My path in all matters to be done   ASTRAL
      For they aspire to the highest kingdom.   CAUSAL

24   If I did not act, these universes would perish,
      For I am mankind's pilot-fish.
      I must act or be the author of confusion
      And of the people the cause of destruction.

25   Arjuna, the unwise act with attachment;
      The wise should act without attachment,
      Seeking to maintain the balance in ascent
      And aiding the world to be well-content.

26   Wise souls, established in Me,
      Should not confuse other entities;
      They should always do their duty
      That other souls might live in beauty.

27   All actions are done by the gunas three.
      The minds of fools, deluded by ego,
      Think that they the truth do know.
      But all is done by the karma of long ago.

28   Arjuna, wise souls of the ego freed,
      Know the difference between the gunas three
      And the innate will of the consciousness tree. — CHAKRAS
      They act unattached, are content to be.

29   Those deluded by the guna flow,
      Becoming attached, run to and fro.
      The wisdom person should never mislead
      The unknowing who are bound by greed.

30   Therefore, dedicate all your actions to Me
      With your mind firmly fixed on the cosmic tree.
      Be free from longing, anxiety and selfishness.
      Cast off thy desire-fever bottomless.

31   Whoever follows My teaching continually;
      Full of confidence, never cowardly,
      Shall be free from karma's bondage eventually;
      And not seeking reward, will find the Lord.

32   Whoever finds fault with this teaching of Mine,
      Will surely not tread the path sublime.
      And in not finding the spiritual gold mine,
      They will ever this earth life malign.

33   All act in conformity to their own nature,
      Both the wise soul and the soul immature.
      All will follow their own inclinations to do;
      Nothing can be gained anew.

34   Attraction and repulsion are only in the mind,   RAGA + DIVESA
      Discerning souls this truth will find.
      Pleasure and pain are the demons of wrath
      Misleading souls on the spiritual path.

35   Better your own duty, though troubling it may be,
      Than another's task, well-performed, glamorously.
      Far better to do your duty and expire;
      By doing another's, great danger you acquire.

36   Krishna, what compels a soul to act foolishly
      Even against its own will, even illogically?
      What compels a soul to short-change its own life
      Driving away self-interest, even causing strife?

37   Arjuna, it is desire, it is wrath
      Begotten of the passion path.
      All consuming, ever-looming
      This is the enemy, ever-booming.

38   As an embryo is covered by a cloak,
      And as fire is enshrouded by smoke,
      As a mirror is hidden by layers of dust,
      So the Spirit is covered by degrees of lust.

39   Arjuna, wisdom is hidden by lust,
      The eternal enemy that the wise distrust.
      The insatiable fire in the form of desire
      Separates the soul from its Holy Sire.

40   The intellect, senses and the mind
      Are the abodes of lust,
      They veil true knowledge from us
      And turn the soul from a state of trust.

41   Regulate the senses, smite down desire;
      Obscure not wisdom with that fire.
      Craving is, indeed, the great destroyer;
      Be thou known as a God Realizer.

42   The senses are greater than the body.
      Greater than the senses is the mind that can see
      And greater than the mind is the consciousness-tree.
      Greater than the greatest is the Life-Breath in Me.

43   Know that which is higher than consciousness,
      Control the lower nest and begin the quest.
      Conquer your enemy called desire,
      Consume the ego in the Holy Fire.

The Yoga of Knowledge

1   Arjuna, I taught the immortal Sun-Deva
     And thus conveyed was the path of Kriya.
     He gave it to his son Manu,
     And Manu imparted it to his son too.

2   This Yoga was handed down to sons
     By royal sages through all the ages.
     Until at last its truth was lost
     As mankind's mind became temper-tossed.

3   This same ancient yoga way
     I impart to you this day.
     Because you are My sincere devotee
     I share with you the supreme mystery.

4   Krishna, how could you have been the first
     To teach the Holy Yoga Verse?
     For I see you are of recent birth
     And the Sun-Deva dates back to antiquity.

5   Arjuna, you and I have lived many births
     This is surely not the first.
     You do not remember the past in the least;
     I remember all, for I am the Supreme Priest.

6   Though unborn, yet am I immortal,
     Lord of all that breathes.
     I manifest through My own divine potency
     For I am always master triumphantly.

7   When goodness grows weak,
     When ignorance is no longer bleak,
     I make and send forth a new body
     To aid and comfort all who seek.

8   In every age I incarnate
     The ignorance of the foolish to abate,
     To give illumination to the holy sage
     And to reestablish the Dharma gauge.

9   That soul who knows the nature
     Of My holy birth and of My task,
     Never again incarnates into pain
     For he walks with Me the holy Dharma lane.

10   Completely rid of passion, fear and wrath,
     Be absorbed in Me and so complete your path.
     Becoming purified by your austerity,
     You will dwell eternally with Me.

11   Whatever a soul asks in devotion,
     That boon I set swiftly into motion.
     On whatever pathway the devoted seek,
     It leads to Me, to them I mystically speak.

12   Most souls worship the Devas for worldly gain,
     But to follow this dream will certainly bring pain.
     The ritual of the mind is the cosmic law,
     So in whatever you seek, see the flaw.

13   The four orders of society I did create.
     I ordered each according to its prenatal trait.
     Yet having authored all that you see
     I, the Eternal Lord, am from the gunas free.

14   Since I have no craving for action's reward,
        I do not take the karmic stain.
        Those who live this law of Mine
        Will never drink the wine of pain.

15   The ancient holy sages of old
        Performed selfless acts of gold;
        And through this path won illumination.
        Arjuna, emulate them in your creation.

16   What is inaction, what is action?
        Even sages are puzzled by this question.
        The truth of this you will shortly know
        And so be released from the karmic flow.

17   Know the truth of the nature of action;
        Understand acts that are not sanctioned.
        Knowing the secrets of inaction be free,
        The mystery of action resides in Me.

18   That soul who sees inaction in action
        And action in inaction
        Is Illumined among mankind;
        That soul is a yogi on the path divine.

19   When all undertakings are free from desire,
        And thoughts purified in the divine fire,
        When actions are consumed by the fire of truth,
        That soul is a sage, the bonds of karma loose.

20   By giving up attachment to action and its fruit,
        You are no longer dependent on the world's root.
        Your soul is then forever satisfied;
        Doing no-thing, yet in action sanctified.

21   By controlling the body and mind,
        You know the Atma, unconfined.
        By renouncing lust and greed,
        You act, but sow not karmic seed.

22   Being content with what comes,
      Being freed from the pairs,
      Pain follows pleasure, you're not confused,
      Gain follows loss, you're not amused.

23   Rid your soul of attachment: be freed.
      Fix your mind on the sacred creed.
      Perform only sacrificial deeds,
      From such actions come the sacred seed.

24   The spiritual offering is the Lord
      The ritual performed is the ancient chord.
      The Lord is the soul acting with ritual accord
      The holy fire is the divine sword.

25   Some souls sacrifice to an astral being
      Others sacrifice to the fire supreme.
      Offer yourself to the stream,
      Become one with God's holy dream.

26   Some sacrifice the process of the senses
      In the fire of self-restraint.
      Others sacrifice the objects of the senses
      And in the fire lose the senses' taint.

27   Those souls seeking Self-realization
      Offer the functions of the senses
      As well as the vital breath
      Into the fire of discipline.

28   Some sacrifice with material things,
      Some with austerity or study,
      Others take a strict vow
      All seek the eternal now.

29   Offering the upward and downward breaths
      As Vishnu's esoteric stance,
      The yogi obtains the holy trance,
      Attaining Samadhi, finding swift advance.

30   Others mortify their flesh and fast
      To free themselves of the body's cast.
      Their sensual fires they turn to ice
      All as holy sacrifice.

31   Of sacrifice these seekers know
      To become free of karma's tow;
      And tasting the nectar of sacrificial food,
      They know the eternal beatitude.

32   All these varied types of sacrifice
      Are approved by the Vedas wise.
      All are rooted in the karma of the mind;
      God finds a place for all in His sacred rhyme.

33   Sacrifice in the form of knowledge
      Is superior to material pledge.
      The end of sacrifice brings alignment
      To the final goal: enlightenment.

34   Prostrate yourself and serve the Guru
      Question him and you will be taught impromptu.
      This self-realized soul can impart wisdom to you
      For such a soul knows That which is true.

35   Arjuna, by acquiring this wisdom-way
      Your mind will no longer be lead astray.
      Know all beings are part of My cosmic sea.
      Love them first there and finally in Me.

36   Though a soul were the foulest of fools,
      Let Knowledge be his footstool,
      And he will pass over the sea of emotion
      By the strong ship of truth's devotion.

37   Arjuna, as a blazing fire
      Reduces wood to ashes and expires,
      So the sacrificial knowledge-fire
      Purges desire and lifts the soul higher.

38   It is this sublime knowledge fire
     That is truly the great purifier.
     The pure heart finds It deep within:
     It is the mature fruit of mysticism.

39   The sincere soul, devoted to wisdom,
     Intent on restraining the senses' collision,
     Finds true joy, abides in Me
     And attains the supreme shanti.

40   Lacking discernment, devoid of devotion,
     A soul knows not positive emotion.
     Such a soul is particularly vexed:
     He can't enjoy this world or the next.

41   That soul who renounces the fruits of action,
     Whose doubts are dissolved by abstraction,
     Who is firmly seated and in control,
     Has no bonds to bind him, for he is whole.

42   I see a doubt still lingers in you
     Because you cannot see what is true.
     Forget the fruits of action this night
     And fight, according to My divine insight.

The Yoga of Action

5

1   Krishna, tell me definitely how
    I may fulfill the sacred vow.
    Of renunciation you so highly speak,
    Yet you ask me the yoga of action to seek.

2   Arjuna, freedom comes
    From action rightly renounced,
    From action rightly begun.
    Both are better than action shunned.

3   Neither hate nor desire action's fruit,
    And you are on the path of the absolute.
    Being liberated from this duality,
    You shall overcome materiality.

4   Some say that action and knowledge are different,
    But those whose lives have not been misspent,
    See knowledge and action as truly one.
    Take either path, the same goal is won.

5   The goal that is gained by wisdom
    Is also reached by the path of action.
    Those souls who see this as true
    Walk the path of Sri Krishna Blue.

6   Without renunciation the soul is chained,
     But with meditation all is gained.
     In quietude you reach the Lord,
     At-one-ment with the wisdom chord.

7   Disciplined by discipline, with purified soul,
     With senses subdued, with self-control,
     Such a soul is dear to everyone then
     And everyone is dear to him.

8   The disciplined soul who knows I never act,
     Knows that action is the guna's impact.
     Wherever he goes, whatever he sees,
     He knows the truth of action in Me.

9   Thus he always knows
     I am not seeing, hearing or touching,
     It is the senses that see and smell.
     To think otherwise keeps the soul in hell.

10   Offering all action to the Lord,
     Shake off attachment, seek not reward.
     Remain untouched by the senses' strain,
     Even as the lotus leaf is untouched by stain.

11   Because the senses are acting alone,
     The disciplined soul must act to atone.
     Abandon attachment with salutation
     For the purpose of self-purification.

12   Disciplined souls leave the fruits of action
     And attain the release of abiding peace.
     The undisciplined act from desire
     Attached to fruits they can never acquire.

13   Renouncing the fruits of passion,
     The soul remains in action.
     Happy is the dweller who thus abates,
     Living in the citadel of the nine gates.

14   Don't say: God gave us this delusion.
      You dream you are in dissolution.
      You dream that action brings evolution;
      It is God's dream that brings the solution.

15   The Master claims not merit or demerit:
      He sacrifices action's fruit.
      Wisdom obscured by craving evolution
      Makes each rebirth a new delusion.

16   But, if by wisdom, delusion be destroyed,
      Then knowledge is no longer a toy.
      Wisdom, like the radiant sun, transubstantiates
      And illuminates the citadel of the nine gates.

17   With mind and heart fixed on My cosmic ocean,
      The final goal is gained by supreme devotion.
      Such souls attain the ultimate goal;
      Ignorance abated, they become whole.

18   The enlightened soul looks non-aghast
      On a higher cast, a cow, an iconoclast.
      With equal dispassion he views life's catalogue:
      An elephant, an outcast, a dog.

19   Being absorbed in the Reality Absolute,
      The sage overrides the irresolute.
      Here in this world he lives and thrives
      And at last at the throne of God arrives.

20   In the Lord abiding, be never backsliding.
      Be ever calm-hearted, thus never tri-parted.
      Not elated by pleasures, not saddened by pains,
      Forever removed are the karmic stains.

21   This soul walks and talks, but is in trance;
      The mind withdrawn from the external dance.
      Completely absorbed, at one with Me,
      He attains My Bliss, he is free.

22   Enjoyments that spring from external contact
      Are wombs bearing sorrow in the zodiac.
      Beginnings and ends to the wheel they cling.
      That which has birth is eternally changing.

23   Even before his departure from earth is due,
      Of every impulse he is a master true.
      Thus he is happy, thus he is free,
      In holy discipline he is one with Me.

24   Only that yogi whose joy is inward,
      Inward his peace, inward his vision,
      Goes to that paradise sun
      Attaining samadhi unison.

25   That soul who is beyond duality and doubt
      Whose mind is inturned and who is devout
      Works for the completion of My dream
      And thereby achieves liberation supreme.

26   Those who have put off desire and wrath
      Those who remain on the unselfish path
      Strive for the fulfillment of My dream
      And find their path in the holy stream.

27   Shut out external objects, raise!
      Focus the gaze past the maze.
      Hold your awareness at the Sun Center, beam!
      Suspend the inward and outward breath-stream.

28   Forsake the relative sense dreams
      And control the mind's extremes.
      Those sages whose goal is final release
      Attain the state of supreme peace.

29   When they know me thus:
      As the author of offering and austerity
      They become planetary Lords with the mystic key
      They become the Lords over materiality.

The Yoga of Meditation

6

1   That soul performing the task dictated by duty,
     Caring not for rewards, is a true yogi.
     But that soul who renounces the sacred fire,
     Will shun action, and not the goal acquire.

2   To abandon all ambition
     And renounce worldly acquisition,
     To drop the dream of the worldly goal
     Is to become a noble soul.

3   The reflective soul, seeking the goal,
     Finds that motiveless action
     Is the holy ladder
     By which he attains the mastery of matter.

4   When, without attachment to action or pleasure,
     You surrender all dreams that you can measure,
     You are said to have attained the yogic soul
     And, in truth, you have reached the goal.

5   A soul should lift itself by its own effort
     And not be debased by excessive sport.
     You can be your own best friend, you see,
     And also your own worst enemy.

6   You are a friend to your own soul
     When the lower self has been made whole.
     But the one not conquering the lower half
     Lives in foolishness, forgets how to laugh.

7   That soul whose mind is perfectly calm
     While living in the stream of opposites,
     In heat or cold, sorrow or joy, can swim
     For the Supreme is established in him.

8   That yogi attuned to wisdom's habitude
     Will have his senses thoroughly subdued.
     Clod, gold or gem break not his self-control.
     He is known as a God-realized soul.

9   He who regards friends and foes, relatives,
     Well-wishers and bearers of fate
     With the equanimity of the spiritual state,
     Transcends the ties of karmic fate.

10   That yogi who subdues his mind and body's desire,
     Freed from things, freed from what he could acquire,
     Lives deep within his spiritual vibration
     And forever engages in Kriya meditation.

11   In a clean place sit in asan firm and fast,
     Make a seat of kusa grass, skin and a cloth at last.
     The seat should be neither too high nor too low
     There you will find your sacred soul.

12   Sitting still, being in concentration,
     Control the mind and its senses
     To reach self-purification;
     Practice yoga for Self-realization.

13   Keep head, trunk, and spine in a straight line,
     In stillness, the secret of Self will unwind;
     Eyes closed, fixed on the bridge of the nose
     Maintain a steady yoga pose.

14   Pledged to a vow of continence,
      Remain calm, fearless, without variance.
      The mind brought under control and fixed on Me
      Is absorbed in samadhi and forever free.

15   Constantly reabsorbing himself in Me
      The yogi transcends materiality.
      Lasting peace and supreme bliss
      Rest in the divine body edifice.

16   Arjuna, this yoga is not for him
      Who eats too much or eats with a whim;
      It is not for one who oversleeps
      Or one who excessive vigil keeps.

17   Yoga, which rids one of woe,
      Is only mastered by that soul aglow,
      Who regulates well diet and play;
      Thus the mind and life go not astray.

18   When the mind is brought under control
      It is focused alone on the Oversoul.
      Freed from yearning for gratification,
      You become established in purification.

19   As flames waver not when sheltered from wind,
      So the mind wavers not when disciplined.
      When the mind is by meditation subdued,
      The soul rejoices, absorbed in God's magnitude.

20   When, through the practice of yoga,
      The mind finally comes to rest
      Content at last to have found the best,
      The soul rejoices, by the Lord is blessed.

21   When the yogi knows that boundless joy
      Ancient wisdom he can then employ
      His awareness is firmly fixed on Me,
      He moves not from truth for he can see.

22   Having felt that boundless peace,
      Truth eternal will never cease;
      A treasure supreme, extending into tomorrow
      A joy not lost by the heaviest sorrow.

23   To firmly achieve this certitude
      Is to gain the real yogic attitude.
      It is breaking the control of pain,
      Thus practice without thought of gain.

24   Renounce all your desires forever
      For they spring from willfulness clever.
      Discern the nature of the world's pretensions
      And restrain your mind's scattering intentions.

25   A soul must be free to attain tranquility,
      Be rid of distraction to gain equanimity.
      Aided by the intelligent will: steadfastness,
      Find peace at last in open-heartedness.

26   Wherever the mind wanders on this earth's clod,
      Draw it gently back to the thought of God.
      However restless the mind appears to be
      Repeatedly recenter your mind on Me.

27   Made utterly quiet by the mind's discipline,
      Made silent by passion's cessation,
      The yogi then knows the Reality,
      His bliss is spirituality.

28   Released from ignorance and without arrogance,
      His mind is constant in contemplation;
      God has touched his meditation.
      Such Bliss is boundless, joyful, without cessation.

29   His heart is with the Lord
      His eye sees only the sacred cord.
      In every creature and in all creation,
      All are blessed by meditation.

30   That yogi who sees Me in all things
     And all things within Me
     Never loses sight of divinity.
     He is in My heart eternally.

31   That yogi who is established in clear seeing
     Worships Me as residing in every being.
     That yogi engages in actions freeing,
     Forever dwelling in Me with well-being.

32   Arjuna, he who sees sameness everywhere,
     Regarding all beings as himself,
     Whether they be in bliss or in pain,
     He knows the highest: all are the same.

33   Krishna, this yoga of peace of soul
     How can it be, even with self-control?
     I do not see how the mind can be stressless
     For the mind is ever so restless.

34   Krishna, restless is the mind emotional,
     In the grip of the senses and non-devotional.
     When gross and grown hard with worldly desire,
     The control of the wind would be easier, sire.

35   Arjuna, the mind is restless, no doubt,
     And difficult to make devout.
     But it can be brought under control
     By constant practice and dispassion of the soul.

36   For a mind uncontrolled and stained,
     The goal of yoga is hard to attain,
     But with self-control and a firm hand
     It is easily reached by methodical plan.

37   Krishna, what happens to the soul
     Whose mind wanders from the goal?
     Will he fail to reach perfection
     What will become of such a perplexed one?

38   When a soul seemingly strays from the Path
       Does he miss both lives, this and the aftermath?
       Where does he find support, how might he rectify,
       Is he lost like a cloud breaking up in the sky?

39   This is the doubt that remains undefined,
       You alone can remove it from my mind.
       Sri Krishna, please answer me now
       Can man fulfill the sacred vow?

40   Arjuna, the defeated soul is never lost
       In this world or the next, he will find the goal.
       No soul who seeks the light to befriend
       Will ever come to a malignant end.

41   Failing to reach the goal of the path,
       He attains the astral in the aftermath,
       And after living on the astral for many years,
       Is born of pious clan and on earth again appears.

42   That soul who fails to reach the yogic goal
       Returns to earth, born of family whole,
       Into parentage of yogis with self-control
       But such a birth is difficult to know.

43   There he gains knowledge from previous lives
       And striving on the Path will thrive.
       Past disciplines cause his path to flower
       He will find Me at the proper hour.

44   But if he takes birth in wealthy family,
       And is held by the power of the senses
       Still he's drawn to God, he'll admit
       By the force of his prenatal habit.

45   By effort and discipline he finds advance
       And is thus purged of all ignorance.
       Through many rebirths that supreme goal
       Is attained by the persistent soul.

46   Arjuna, find the master key:
Be in union with God, be a yogi.
Be greater than they mortifying earthly sheath,
Doers of good works, or they who knowledge seek.

47   That yogi who gives Me all his heart
Attuning to Me and never apart,
That soul among all others I call My very own;
Even though unlettered, that soul can be unfettered.

The Yoga of Realization

7

1 Arjuna, dedicate your mind and soul to Me
   Practice the yoga of simplicity.
   Take Me for your only real comfort
   And you will know of My total support.

2 I will give you all knowledge of the soul
   Direct vision will make you whole.
   When a soul thus experiences and sees
   Nothing remains that it wishes to be.

3 Of those souls who seek to be
   Only one in a thousand will find Me.
   And of those who have the power of seeing
   Perchance only one knows My total being.

4 Divided into air, earth, water and fire,
   Space, intellect, mind and ego desire,
   Dividing thus, making eight,
   Does My true nature separate.

5 Other than this nature, which is low,
   My higher being you must know:
   My higher life by which all is sustained
   And by which the material world is maintained.

6   All beings have their origin in My mystic verse,
     Have evolved from My nature, are made anew,
     For I am the source of this universe
     And I am its dissolution too.

7   In all of life there is no thing
     Superior to My cosmic ring.
     The universes are strung on the Lord
     Just as perfect pearls on a silken cord.

8   I am the essence of water,
     Of the Sun and Moon I am the light.
     I am the sacred mantra of the Vedas bright,
     The sound in space and manhood's might.

9   I am the fragrance of the earth
     I am life that gives birth.
     I am the brilliance that appears in the fire
     The austerity in men without desire.

10   I am the seed in every being
     I am the mind of enlightened seeing.
     The eternal ones know assuredly
     I am the glory in the cosmic melody.

11   I am the might that dwells in the mighty,
     Freed from lust and longings' fire.
     And where the law has not forbidden,
     Within all creatures I am that desire.

12   Whatever comes from goodness,
     Know that comes from Me, the limitless.
     Those of darkness or of passion begot
     Dwell in Me, but I am in them not.

13   By these three guna qualities
     The worlds are led astray.
     Thus most fail to recognize today
     That I am changeless and greater than they.

14   For this is My cosmic Maya
     Born of the gunas three.
     The soul who trusts in Me and My decree
     Holds fast to wisdom and in Maya is free.

15   Degraded souls, lost in ignorance,
     Do not embrace Me, do not advance;
     Stripped of wisdom, in delusion they groan,
     Held to negativity they walk alone.

16   Four kinds of souls attune to Me:
     Those who suffer and those who aspire
     Brought to their lot by karmic desire,
     Then the wise who know and the good who grow.

17   The wise soul who loves unity excels
     And in constant meditation dwells.
     To that wise soul I am the Overlord
     With Me that noble one is in accord.

18   All of these are noble in austerity,
     But I consider as My very own soul
     The one who comes to Me whole
     Seeking Me alone as the highest goal.

19   And at the end of many a rebirth,
     Through meditation his discernment grows
     Til at last he knows, Vasudeva is all
     How great and rare is such a soul.

20   But souls who are tossed on the waves of desire
     Bound by their egos from rising higher,
     Adopt various relative religious rules
     Place trust in other forces and become cruel.

21   Worship any god you please,
     I enter the heart of the devotee.
     Attune in faith and purity,
     Know that I will answer lovingly.

22   If disciplined by that attunement,
       You propitiate the deities for gain
       And if you acquire all your desires
       It is because I Myself have so ordained.

23   When your prayers are small and ego-bound
       You have not found the unchanging ground.
       To the devas you will go, if the devas you please
       But to Me, finally, come My devotees.

24   I am unmanifest and forever without form
       But foolish souls seek Me in the body dream.
       They do not know of My higher nest:
       The unchanging, the Supreme.

25   I am to all souls not revealed
       For by My Maya am I concealed.
       Even those who perceived Me forgot
       That fixed forever, I change not.

26   I know the beings of the past
       And everyone of present time;
       I know the beings yet to be
       Yet so few souls know Me.

27   Delusion arising from duality
       Produces desire and aversion,
       Confuses every soul on earth
       From the moment of their birth.

28   Those souls of meritorious deed
       Whose karma has returned to seed,
       Love Me with steadfast mind and creed
       And from the pairing they are freed.

29   That soul who strives and relies on Me
       Is released, he shall be free.
       He knows the Reality as a whole
       And the karmic secrets of the soul.

30   Those souls who know Me
     In beings, gods and every act,
     Find that at the hour of their passing
     They rest in Me, the Everlasting.

The Yoga of the
Eternal Reality

8

1   Krishna, who is the Reality, what is Spirit
Why is karma, when is substance linked to it
How do the Devas these things define
Where is ultimate power divine?

2   How does the law of reciprocity function
What is the way to face death's corruption
How do the Devas prove these things so
Can self-controlled souls truly know?

3   Arjuna, Reality is perfect changelessness
Spirit is self-perpetuation, timelessness
Karma is that which is inborn in the soul
It is these three which create the whole.

4   Materiality is that which changes
Divine Power is bodiless as It ranges.
The law of reciprocity dreamt
Is your own present embodiment.

5   Whoever at the time of death's release
Consciously leaves the body's reach,
And attuning to Me alone meditates
Will surely come to My holy state.

6   Whatever tendencies you hold in mind
     When at death you leave your body aside,
     That very state you will find
     For an astral lifetime there abide.

7   Center your awareness on Me and fight;
     Attune to Me and do what is right.
     With reason and devotion bend your knee
     And you will most certainly come to Me.

8   Uninterruptedly committed to the soul
     Ever hold your mind to the great goal.
     Be not attached to anything, do not deviate
     Merge with the power by which all life is animate.

9   Balanced Awareness is what It is called,
     Unthinkable in shape and smaller than the small.
     He who meditates on God beyond the judgment hall
     Sees the Lord, sun-colored, the establisher of all.

10   With mind unmoving at death's departure time,
     Holding the breath between the eyebrow space
     Devotion and yoga vision embrace
     Thus find the Lord, the Highest Divine Grace.

11   Knowers of Truth seek the supreme goal,
     Indestructible harmony of the soul.
     These ascetics have their passions spent
     To show this sacred state is My sole intent.

12   When a soul closes all the body's doors,
     Not allowing the sacred breath to depart,
     And holding the mind within the heart,
     Practice Samadhi, wisdom to impart.

13   Remember Me always, chant My sacred Om!
     Thus you will leave the body's home.
     And tasting the path of the honeycomb,
     You will walk the way to the cosmic dome.

14   By thinking of the Lord incessantly
      And by attuning the mind to Me alone,
      The soul of constant discipline
      Learns I am not hard to win.

15   Great souls who have found solace in Me
      Have left the lonely place of misery.
      And gaining at last My supreme emanation
      They have not the need for reincarnation.

16   The spheres as high as Brahma's realm
      Dissolve, you see, and then return to be.
      But whoever comes to Me is the unseeded
      And no more is transmigration needed.

17   Such souls know that the Day of Brahma
      A thousand ages will last
      And each night an equal time will pass;
      Thus they know how these cycles are amassed.

18   All manifested things spring forth, they say,
      At each and every birth of Brahma's Day.
      All things dissolve again at Brahma's Night
      Back, back into the unmanifested light.

19   The whole range of beings on this cosmic ball
      Helplessly dissolve at Brahma's nightfall.
      And over and over again must appear
      Forming anew when Brahma's Day is here.

20   There is an ultimate mode of existence
      Unmanifested beyond the unmanifest.
      Know that when everything is totally void
      This primal origin will not be destroyed.

21   This Supreme Unmanifest is My royal throne,
      Once attained, forever home.
      Great souls say It is the highest road
      For It is My supreme Supreme Abode.

22   This then is the Highest Spirit,
       All lesser souls are held in It.
       Know that love alone propitiates;
       All the universes I permeate.

23   I will now inform you of the places and times
       In the astral where the yogi climbs,
       The realms in which he does sojourn
       And I will speak of the times of no-return.

24   In the six months of the Sun's northern way,
       In fire, light and bright moon or day,
       Those souls who depart at this hour
       Ascend to God's Sun, they hold Divine Power.

25   In the six months of the Sun's southern path,
       In smoke, night, new moon or darkness,
       Those who leave at this time attain the moon
       And return again to the bodily room.

26   These paths of sun light and of darkness saturn
       Form an eternal cosmic pattern;
       One for the soul who has yet to learn
       And one for the path of no-return.

27   And knowing of this secret course
       The yogi is led not into remorse,
       For he is always balanced therein
       By means of meditative discipline.

28   Whatever merit-fruit the rishis ordain:
       Scriptures, alms, rituals or ascetic pain,
       The disciplined yogi knows that secret way
       And ascends to the Lord in that Holy Day.

The Yoga of the
Royal Pathway

9

1   As Life's Goodness to you is not concealed,
     The greater mystery I shall now reveal
     Innermost secret, knowledge of God's wheel
     This wisdom shall free you to bear My seal.

2   This knowledge brings instant liberation
     It is a sovereign science, the holy equation.
     Nearer than knowing, open vision,
     Direct and holy premonition.

3   Those who know not attunement
     Have not My royal knowledge found,
     And not attaining My form, they are bound
     On the karmic wheel they spin around.

4   The total cosmos by Me is pervaded
     Even as ice by water is mated.
     In Me all things must truly subsist
     Though we coexist, I pre-exist.

5   Created things are not present in Me
     Such is the force of My mystery.
     I create and sustain endlessly;
     Not dependent on things, I am free.

6   As the wind's all-pervading race
     Is forever dependent upon space,
     So do all things depend on Me
     In my form dwells the duality.

7   At the very end of every age
     All things dissolve from their cage
     And at the beginning of every age
     I recreate them across life's page.

8   Helpless are they for Maya is their master,
     But I am of this Maya, Lord.
     Again and again I send forth these multitudes
     From Me they spring creating life's vicissitudes.

9   How shall these creations bind Me
     For I am detached, from gain unlatched.
     I stand as the Watcher on the Hill
     Watching Maya and mankind's free will.

10   Maya creates all: the motionless and the moving.
     Arjuna, this is why the cosmos is orbiting,
     Turning its wheel through dissolution
     As well as through rebirth's solution.

11   Foolish souls despise Me
     When I take on the human guise;
     For they are blind to My highest state
     As Lord of Being, the great cosmic slate.

12   Vain their hope and vain their labor,
     Void of knowledge, the truth they abhor.
     And holding fiendish thoughts that betray
     They embrace the way that leads astray.

13   Great are they who become godlike, breathless;
     They alone know Me, the birthless, the deathless.
     These souls offer Me the motiveless homage,
     A sincere unwavering conscious pledge.

14   These souls glorify Me constantly,
      Showing meditative love consistently
      With great zeal and steadfast vow,
      In devotion to Me they humbly bow.

15   Some worship Me knowing God is in all and great.
      Some see Me as one with them, others as separate.
      Many bow to countless gods in different places,
      These are but My billion pure divine faces.

16   I am the holy rite, I am the sacrifice,
      I am the fire and the offering;
      Also the herb and the gift to the dead;
      I am the butter and the mantra said.

17   I am the Lord of the world, the unifier,
      The known, the knowing, the purifier,
      The mother, the founder and the home,
      The three sacred books and the holy Om.

18   I am the goal and the path,
      The source, sustainer and Lord without wrath,
      The friend, witness and refuge in need,
      The treasure house and the changeless seed.

19   I am the warmth of the sun and fire
      I am death and life's first sire
      I let loose the rain and I restrain
      I am the cosmos revealed and the sacred reign.

20   The soma drinkers offer Me sacrifice,
      Believe in the three scriptures and seek paradise.
      Purified, they swim the astral streams
      And sup upon the deva's highest dreams.

21   When the soul's good karma is spent,
      It falls from the astral plane
      And again regains the earthly stain.
      Thus souls become bound in pain.

22   To those souls who attune to Me alone
      I bring the blessing to gain the unsown
      Who truly serve Me and persevere,
      I gather and guard what they gain here.

23   When with faith to other gods, souls offer honestly
      Though not in ways the law decrees,
      Still, they of other gods are devotees
      Pure are they, for gods are the fruit of My tree.

24   I am the true Lord, I am the all,
      The receiver of sacrifice large and small.
      Those souls who do not recognize Me
      In the pattern of life are never free.

25   Ancestor worshipers go to their ancestors
      Seekers of elemental spirits receive astral visitors
      Offer to any deity and that deity you attain
      Those who serve Me shall come to Me again.

26   Whatever a noble soul to Me does bring,
      Fruit, water, flower or leaf offering,
      Because of that soul's devotion I accept it
      That gift is love, the heart's dedicated rite.

27   Arjuna, whatever you do, wherever you run
      Whatever the obligation or austerity done
      Whatever the gift to mankind you present
      Offer all as sacrifice and on Me be intent.

28   With mind established in renunciation,
      Be free from bonds of good and bad adulteration.
      Practice meditative discipline the Spirit to see,
      The end in itself, become one with Me.

29   I am equally present in all beings
      There are none hateful or dear to My heart strings.
      Whoever succors to Me, in Me abides
      And thus the Lord Within never hides.

30   Though a soul through a lifetime be soiled
With total ignorance uncoiled,
If that soul but love Me with right constraint,
I see no soil, no taint, that soul is a saint.

31   Speedily does that soul become holy
And holiness soon refashions his passions
He attains wisdom and eternal peace
Every true disciple will gain release.

32   All who find in Me a shelter cave
The ignorant, the foolish, the mental slave
Including those whose birth is low,
The highest attainment even they can know.

33   The path for holy priests in all ages
Is to find the truth of the royal sages.
And having attained this divine eloquence,
Seek out Illumination with great diligence.

34   Make all your actions acts of abnegation,
Bowing down in ego-abnegation.
On Me your heart, on Me your mind,
And surely, swiftly the Lord you will find.

The Yoga of Sacred Splendor

10

1   Arjuna, you shall hear My highest word
    For my call you have heard.
    Listen to this that I shall tell
    For I sincerely wish you well.

2   Neither devas nor sages know the secret
    Of My incarnation in human silhouette.
    I am the source that continually converges
    Into the sustaining of all that emerges.

3   Who knows Me as the omnipotent,
    The unborn, the undying, the changeless,
    That mortal soul alone becomes stainless
    And from every ill distills good will.

4   All traits from Me arise
    Fear or forgiveness, even lies
    The peace, pain and patience in dying
    The fearlessness of once-more trying.

5   Truth brings pure enlightenment
    From self-control comes detachment.
    In ill-repute or fame be harmless
    Such knowledge makes a soul bounteous.

6   The seven sages and then the ancient four
      Were the astral offspring of My interior.
      And the worldly creatures sprang from those
      Til at last the fourteen Manus rose.

7   Who knows My supreme glory
      Is balanced most certainly.
      He knows the force which works therein
      Because of total discipline.

8   l am the origin in all things,
      The issuing-forth of all beings.
      Known through attunement by the wise
      Who fully love without compromise.

9   With their life totally absorbed in Me
      They teach of their Lord constantly.
      They offer to one another My Light
      For they find in Me the true delight.

10   To those souls who are always disciplined,
      Who show Me true love from deep within,
      I give to them the balanced consciousness
      Through Me they attain absoluteness.

11   I dispel the darkness born of ignorance,
      My shining lamp is their inheritance.
      With kindliness their karma I dissipate
      Yet I remain balanced in My Own Cosmic State.

12   Krishna, you are the Reality, the most exquisite,
      The utterly holy, the primal spirit,
      Lord Eternal, the uplifter, the all-excelling,
      Divine, unborn, our highest dwelling.

13   All sages have proclaimed you birthless.
      Narada, Devala and Asita so declare
      That you are the ancient heavenly seer.
      Now before me this secret you swear.

14   Beloved Krishna, now I see
      The truth you have revealed to me:
      Angels and demons are unaware
      That your holy form is everywhere.

15   Creator of all beings, ruler of all creatures,
      Lord of lords, God of gods, Spirit of all scriptures,
      Supreme Spirit, you alone comprehend
      How unmanifest you are manifest within.

16   Your divine powers are all-pervading
      Your own self is all-envisioning,
      And yet you forever remain the same
      I pray for me this truth you will frame.

17   Oh, master of yoga, how am I to know Thee?
      How may you be totally realized by me?
      Am I to know Thee through constant meditation,
      Or through various states of being edification?

18   Krishna, tell me again in fullest delight
      Of your divine potency, your cosmic might.
      To know again that joy as first I heard
      The holy nectar of your deathless word.

19   Arjuna, my chief powers I will explain to you,
      For of the lesser permutations there is no end.
      My divine all-pervading powers I transcend,
      For unbounded through space and time I extend.

20   I am in the heart of every being
      I am the origin and the midst of things
      I am also their final end as well
      I am the Atma installed therein to dwell.

21   I am Vishnu among the twelve sons
      I am Marichi of the wind devas
      I am the bright-rayed solar sun of light
      I am the moon among the stars of night.

22   I am Indra among the astral beings
      I am the mind among the senses
      I am Sama of the Vedas taught
      And in all beings I am thought.

23   I am Shiva of the astral death-fire
      I am the fire in brilliant Vasu's attire
      I am the Lord of Wealth, of all who seek
      And Mount Meru of all the mountain peaks.

24   I am chief among the arch priests
      I am Skanda of the warrior beasts
      The Lord Brihaspati is in Me
      And of the waters, I am the cosmic sea.

25   Of all the sages, I am Sri Bhrigu rare
      Of acts of worship, I am the mantric prayer
      Among sounds, I am the sacred Om syllable
      I am the Himalaya of things unmovable.

26   I am the holy Bo of all the trees
      I am Chitra-ratha who does please
      I am Sri Narada of seers divine
      And the wise Kapila of perfect line.

27   Among horses, I am Indra's steed
      Sprung forth from the nectarian seaweed
      Of royal elephants, I am majestic
      And King of kings among mortal men domestic.

28   I am the Lord of love's creating fire
      Of sacred cows, I am the wish-fulfiller
      Of weapons, I am the thunderbolt that shakes
      And I am the cobra, king of snakes.

29   I am Ananta of mystical folklores
      I am the Ancient One among the ancestors
      I am the watery deva of the watery being
      And I am death, the all decreeing.

30   I am Prahlada among the demons
Of those who measure, I am time's cones
I am Vishnu's eagle among birds that take wing
And among all animals, I am their king.

31   I am the Ganges among all the rivers
I am the Rama of the warriors
The Leviathan of the waters am I
And the good wind that doth sanctify.

32   The very beginning of creation am I
I am Shiva's end and Vishnu's preservation
I am that which is attained through self-control
And of knowledge, I am the science of the soul.

33   Among the letters, "A," I am
And of compound words I am, I AM.
I am truly immortal time
The ordainer filling space with rhyme.

34   I am the Gayatri that unbinds
I am the archer, first among the signs
I am the greatest chant that souls can sing
And of the seasons, I am spring.

35   I am death that carries all away, you see,
I am the origin and source of things to be
I am the goddess of wisdom and fame
Patience, steadfastness and memory are My name.

36   I am conquest, I am Godlihood
I am the good of the good.
I am the dice of those who speculate
I am the greatness of the great.

37   I am Vasudeva of my clan
And Sri Vyasa the hermit man
I am you, Arjuna, of Pandu's sons
And wise Shirka of the thoughtful ones.

38   I am the statecraft of the cabinet
      I am the silence of the secret
      I am the rod through which men chastise
      And I am the wisdom of the wise.

39   I am whatever is of seed
      In every kind of being its need
      Without Me nothing can exist,
      Without Me there is no bliss.

40   The truth from you I shall not hide
      So I have My primary powers described.
      As I have said, they shall never end
      For into eternity they extend.

41   Life is a boundless mystery
      The universes revolve in My Majesty.
      Life's brilliance, grandeur and powerful might
      Come from a spark of My own divine light.

42   But what is the gain, all this to know?
      Suffice it to say I am the energy flow.
      The whirling cosmos I sustain
      With but a spark, yet full I remain!

The Yoga of the Mystical Vision

11

1   Krishna, in compassion you have revealed
    In whole the wisdom nature of the soul.
    Your words resounding life's deepest mystery
    Have banished my mind's perplexity.

2   Of the origin and the dissolution
    You spoke in detail with just elocution.
    The nature of all creatures I have learned in full
    Even of your own soul unchangeable.

3   You are as you describe yourself to be
    The truth of this I clearly see.
    However, Krishna, I wish to behold
    Your cosmic form of dazzling gold.

4   Oh, Lord of mystic vision reveal to me
    Thy immortal and glorious Omnic Tree.
    Grant the vision that I might see
    Who you are to life and to me.

5   Arjuna, behold by hundreds and thousands
    The celestial devas of various kinds;
    Now see My cosmic form displayed
    In ever-changing shape and shade.

6   See the devas twin-born to heal
     Devas of light, sun and breath-storm with zeal,
     Lords of Return and many marvels more
     By earthlings never seen before.

7   This very day you shall behold
     The whole universe within My soul.
     Within this body composed of one limb,
     See what you wish for I am your friend.

8   But you cannot see My cosmic display
     With those gross eyes of material clay.
     So I give unto you the single eye
     To see your very Lord thereby.

9   Sanjaya said: Having spoken the heavenly word
     Sri Krishna, the sage of all yogas bestirred
     And in mystic vision revealed to Arjuna
     His divine, holy cosmic vertebra.

10   Krishna's form has countless cosmic views
     With heavenly weapons of various hues.
     The Lord has many a mouth and many a single eye
     He bore celestial ornaments as are worn on high.

11   Garlands and infinite holy robes He wore,
     Wondrous sandalwood scents He bore.
     This Cosmic Lord with dazzling display
     Faced everywhere: to the night, to the day.

12   If ever in the heavens there did come
     The mighty splendor of a thousand suns,
     That would hardly resemble the golden whole
     That is the glory of God's cosmic soul.

13   In the single body of the Lord of the Lord
     The cosmos converged into one polychord.
     Arjuna could now altogether behold
     How the universe is divided many-fold.

14   Thus Arjuna, with hair standing on end,
      Filled with awe, filled with wonder then
      Bowed his head toward the Lord of Thunder
      And with palms joined said to the Untread:

15   Oh, Lord I see within that cosmic form of thine
      That each deva, each being doth shine.
      Lord Shiva and Lord Brahma upon his Lotus throne,
      All seers, all nagas, even the foundation stone.

16   With eyes, arms, bellies and mouths manifold,
      I see Thy endless form of all unfold.
      I see no beginning, midst or end of Thee
      Yet in each form I see your Omnic Tree.

17   Thy diadem, rod and chakra I clearly see.
      You shine on every side like the primordial sea.
      You are a sphere of divine brilliancy
      In glorious flames as fire flames immeasurably.

18   You are the eternal joyous indestructible beam,
      The highest wisdom, the abiding place supreme
      The changeless guardian of the eternal right,
      The everlasting spirit of the imperishable light.

19   Infinite your arms, the sun and moon your eyes,
      Thy flaming mouth galactically rectifies.
      Without beginning or end you are the cosmic might.
      With celestial radiance you bring the worlds to light.

20   Your glory fills space on every side,
      The four quadrants are by you occupied.
      Seeing these wondrous, yet awesome forms flexed,
      All the planetary systems stand perplexed.

21   Hosts of devas are now entering you aflame,
      Some, palms pressed out in fear, sing your name.
      Great sages and ones-of-power chant, "Shanti"
      Worshipping your form as whirling dharmic sea.

22   All the twelve great groups and their rays
      Do ever seek you and ever on you gaze.
      Devas, manes, rishis and men sing praise;
      As they behold Thee, they stand amazed.

23   Thy mighty cosmic form has many a mouth and eye,
      Great with many arms, feet and mighty thighs,
      Great with many bellies, and grim with many teeth
      The three worlds see this and quake, and I also shake.

24   Oh Vishnu, seeing Thy Cosmic Form,
      I have lost my peace and steadiness,
      For vast are Thy gaping mouths
      And huge Thy eyes of fierceness.

25   Seeing Your face with mouths of fire,
      Jagged teeth, the dissolution pyre,
      I have lost the direction of the sky.
      Be merciful, where does the center lie!

26   The Blind King's sons and hosts of other kings
      Bhisma, Drona and the son of Karna too,
      Along with our own noble warriors
      Rush into Your wide fanged jaws in horror.

27   Into Thy open mouths they quickly rush,
      Some are seen—their heads are crushed,
      And some are lodged between Thy teeth,
      Their cries are harrowing cries of grief.

28   Just as flooded streams from bonds break free
      Rushing swiftly downward toward the one great sea,
      So charge these warriors of the human realm
      In Thy gaping mouths are they overwhelmed.

29   As moths fly rapidly taking aim
      To meet their end in the burning flame,
      So all the worlds impulsively draw near,
      And rush to Thy mouth, their funeral bier.

30   Gulping whole worlds from every turn,
      How does Your dreadful splendor burn!
      Devouring all in jaws blazing wide,
      Yet throughout the Cosmos are You glorified!

31   Oh, One of Awesome Form, who truly art thou?
      Oh Lord of All, have compassion as I bow.
      I wish to know Thee and Thy purpose,
      To comprehend Thy metempsychosis.

32   Lo, I am Inflamed Time, I cause the worlds to decay.
      I mature and resolve the worlds I take away.
      Arjuna, you have your part to play
      As do these soldiers in the battle array.

33   And so, Arjuna, arise to a triumphant glory
      Defeat your foe, enjoy meaningful victory.
      These soldiers by Me are already slain
      You are but an instrument of life's aim.

34   You but smite the dead, the doom-devoted heroes,
      Jaya-dratha, Drona, Bhisma and Karna overthrow.
      Strike down these warriors in the battle today
      Fight and defeat your foes in the fray.

35   With palms pressed and trembling at Krishna's word,
      Arjuna prostrated, his soul was stirred.
      He again did homage to Lord Krishna and spoke
      In faltering, stammering voice did he choke:

36   Lord, the worlds offer you praise
      Chanting your name in various ways.
      All the enlightened host do you homage pay
      And demons flee to the outermost maze.

37   Oh, Lord, these worlds should you adore
      Greater than Brahma, greater than first progenitor,
      The imperishable, the non-being, the ancient lore,
      The Lord of Celestials, the abode of terrestrials.

38   You are the primal Lord, the great ancient soul,
      The eternal abiding place for the whole.
      The known, the knowing, the greatest goal
      The formless form pervading life's noble scroll.

39   Wind and water, fire and death are Thee
      Also the moon, the ancestor and creator I see.
      To Thee all love and homage ever be
      To Thee all love and homage, set us free.

40   All love to Thee, Lord of every quadrant.
      All love to Thee in front and from behind.
      All love to Thee, to Thee be homage unconfined.
      You are all-fulfilling, all exists in Thee I find.

41   Carelessly I called you "Krishna" and "My Friend"
      I was overbold, love-filled without end
      Unaware of your majestic majesty, did I offend
      As I mistook you for a mortal friend?

42   Lord, if I showed Thee disrespect in jest,
      While playing, walking, eating or at rest,
      While alone or in the midst of the throng,
      If I did wrong, forgive me, hear my song.

43   Author of these worlds, of all things motionless,
      Of all moving beings, greatest teacher whom we bless,
      In the three universes none equals Thee,
      You are unexcelled in holy majesty.

44   Sri Krishna, at your feet I prostrate low
      Sri Krishna, Thy holy grace do now bestow.
      As a friend, sweet compassion show,
      Forgive me as a father does his son.

45   What no earth soul has ever seen, now I see.
      Lord of Celestials, be compassionate with me.
      My heart is thrilled, my mind a raging storm.
      Again, Oh Lord, show me Thy four-armed form.

46 Adorned with diadem, rod and chakra that you bore
    I wish to see you as you were before.
    Oh thousand-armed one of the universal shore,
    Show unto me your four-armed shape once more.

47 Arjuna, out of My love for you I have shown
    My highest form, fire with endless splendor,
    Manifested by yoga-power of My Om,
    Which no earthling before has ever known.

48 No one before has seen my Universal Form
    Not through study of scriptures, sacrifice or fees,
    Nor by ritual or by strict austerity.
    Arjuna, only you have seen My Fleur-de-lis.

49 Arjuna, be not alarmed, abate your senseless fear,
    Be not bewildered, be of good cheer.
    Holding conch, rod, chakra and lotus I appear.
    Behold, I take again My four-armed form right here!

50 Thus to Arjuna, Lord Vasudeva declared the whole
    And the fearful Arjuna he did console.
    He took again His natural four-armed form
    As Lord Krishna, the Holy-Born.

51 Krishna, now that I see Your gracious human form
    I can once more calmly contemplate
    For my gross senses are balancing and
    Returning to their normal state.

52 Arjuna, this galactic Form which you observed
    Is exceedingly difficult to see.
    This is the Holy Form the devas long to see
    In sacred vision constantly.

53 Neither by study of scripture,
    Nor by penitence, alms or sacrifice,
    Nor by ritual can I be known in whole
    As you have seen My Mystic Form unfold.

54   Only by attuned love
      Can I be known and entered in above.
      Only by single-minded devotion
      Can I be seen as the One-in-Motion.

55   Arjuna, work for Me, be intent on Me;
      Be free from ties, from lies, have love for Me.
      And without hate for any creature whatsoever,
      You shall, oh royal prince, dwell with Me forever.

The Yoga of Devotion

12

1   Krishna, some attune to You the manifest
     Some attune to God the changeless, the unmanifest.
     Which discipline is the most favorable;
     Which path leads to the bountiful?

2   Arjuna, souls who concentrate on a form of Mine,
     Unselfishly serving, determined to climb,
     Are pervaded with attunement whole
     Thus they are able to grasp life's goal.

3   But to those who attune to the unmanifest,
     The unformed, the unthinkable, the best,
     The fixed, the imperishable, the unconfined,
     The unchanging and the undefined,

4   Those souls truly enjoy tranquility,
     Are devoted to doing good to all in Me.
     All the senses they ever restrain
     Thus My True Self they fully attain.

5   The Unmanifest is more difficult to attain
     For the embodied seek form again and again.
     It is extremely difficult for a soul
     To touch and attain this unmanifest goal.

6   To those souls who cast their cares on Me,
     Who have silent and undivided discipline,
     Who do everything for Me and quietly wait
     They will revere My form as they meditate.

7   To those souls whose attention is centered on Me,
     I am the swift deliverer from the mortal sea.
     I am immediately and automatically found
     Ending their rebirth cycle, the transmigrating round.

8   Arouse your soul to be absorbed in Me.
     Lodge your mind in Me, dwell in Me,
     Fix your meditative mind on Me alone
     And you will truly find Me, the Cosmic Om.

9   If you cannot be absorbed in My form steadily,
     Then practice concentration-of-thought on Me.
     Through the withdrawal of thought realize Me
     By the holy discipline of yoga be free.

10   But if you lack the power to concentrate,
     Then perform good works for My sake.
     Please Me in your every action
     And you will find your perfection.

11   But if you are unable to do even this,
     Then surrender to Me, life's edifice.
     Control the desires of your heart: abstain,
     Renounce all fruits, be self-restrained.

12   Knowledge is better than mere mental exercise.
     Meditation is definitely more than wise.
     Detachment from fruits is above meditation,
     From detachment comes Illumination.

13   Do not hate any living animal
     But be friendly and compassionate to all.
     Be released from your ego selfishness
     Be ever the same in pain or happiness.

14   The disciplined soul who remains content,
      With his thoughts and feelings on Me intent
      He is, indeed, self-controlled, full grown
      He is My disciple, he is My Own.

15   That soul by the world is not disturbed,
      By the world that soul is never perturbed.
      Freed from fear and envy, he does not groan,
      Anxiety abated, he is My Own.

16   Balanced and thus craving for nothing
      Ready for all, not perturbed by anything
      Able to deal with the unexpected alone
      Neither vain nor anxious, he is My Own.

17   That soul who neither loves nor loathes,
      That soul who neither grieves nor craves
      For that which is sown or unsown
      Is truly balanced, he is My Own.

18   His attitude is equal toward foe or friend,
      Fame and obscurity he transcends.
      Freed from heat, cold, pleasure and harassment,
      He is truly detached from attachment.

19   Equally detached being praised or blamed,
      Content with what comes and with tongue tamed,
      His home is everywhere and his mind full-grown;
      Filled with devotion, he is My Own!

20   Partaking fully of this nectarian wisdom,
      Practicing constantly with true devotion,
      Intent on My Form, placing Me on his throne;
      He is My disciple, he is truly My Own!

The Yoga of the Karma Field

13

What is the difference between Spirit and matter,
Between the field and its Holy Knower,
Between knowledge and that which is known,
Between the sower and that which is sown?

1   Arjuna, this body and nature are called the field
     Because seeds of action are sown therein.
     That which sees what the harvest-field yields
     Is called by sages the Knower of the Field.

2   Know Me as the knower of this field diverse
     Dwelling in everyone in the Universe.
     I regard the discernment between the field
     And the Knower to be wisdom's highest yield.

3   What is the field and what is its nature;
     Who is the Knower and what is His signature?
     What its changes are and how they come to be,
     You shall soon understand this mystery from Me.

4   The ancient sages have expressed this truth
     In many a hymn and many an aphorism,
     And also in many a spiritual verse
     They taught the Truth in ways diverse.

5   Primordial matter evolved into intellect and ego,
     Then the ten organs of action and ways to know.
     Then came the mind and the five subtle elements,
     Then the five objects of sensual discernment.

6   The field is now succinctly described:
     Desire, aversion, pleasure, pain and pride,
     Awareness, perception and their continuance
     Constitute the field and its substance.

7   Be thou humble, be thou harmless
     And serve your guru in selflessness.
     With patience and purity of body and mind,
     Be self-controlled with steadiness divine.

8   Be thou detached from objects of sense,
     Understand the true nature of providence:
     Of birth, disease, old age and death,
     And bring at least to rest your breath.

9   Be thou detached, with no excessive desire,
     Acquire the state of constant balance,
     Though sons, spouse or blessed home
     Come to you, stay or choose to roam.

10   With devotion to My form crystalline,
     Attain single-minded yogic discipline.
     Dwell quietly in sacred solitude
     Far from the noise of the multitude.

11   Seek wisdom that concerns the soul,
     Learn that truth which leads to the goal.
     Gain wisdom to remove your ignorance
     For all else is simply arrogance.

12   Knowing the Reality in fullest degree,
     You will attain conscious immortality
     And will be released from all your fears;
     Know Me, balanced between the hemispheres.

13   Its hands, feet and head are everywhere.
      It embraces everything in the world out there.
      It has eyes, ears and mouths on all sides,
      It fills all things, yet It singly abides.

14   It is the perceiver of all objects dense
      But is itself devoid of every sense.
      It is unattached and without a strand,
      Yet It is the enjoyer of all that is grand.

15   External and internal, yet eternal in each being,
      Utterly distant, yet ever near through clear-seeing;
      It lives in the moving and in the motionless,
      It is beyond mind's grasp because of Its subtleness.

16   Undivided, It seems to divide.
      Sending forth Its creation, It abides.
      It should be known as That which creates
      And also consumes and animates.

17   This is the Light of all light,
      The knowledge, the known and the goal outright.
      "Beyond the Darkness" It is called
      Established in the heart of one and all.

18   You now have knowledge of the field and its yield.
      The devotee who truly comprehends this field,
      The knowledge and the known, I declare,
      My own state of being that soul shall share.

19   Arjuna, know that matter and spirit
      Are equally without beginning,
      But the triple strands and all the changes
      Come from matter which constantly rearranges.

20   In cause, effect or agency,
      Matter is known as the cause to be.
      In pleasure, pain, rejection or applause,
      The Spirit is known as the experiencing cause.

21   The Spirit, when seated in the material container,
      Tastes objects from strands born of matter.
      Attachment to these strands produces desire
      And thus rebirth in bodies does transpire.

22   Spirit, when dwelling in this human container,
      Is yet transcendent, still is free.
      Spirit is the witness, guide and sustainer
      It is the oversoul, the supreme majestic decree.

23   Arjuna, that soul who knows of the Spirit
      And of nature with its qualities,
      Despite its karma or state of being,
      Will not be reborn, but will find the freeing.

24   Some, by meditation in their own heart,
      Behold the True Self by the pure-reason dart.
      Others behold It by treading the knowledge-path
      Others know the Spirit through the action path.

25   Then there are those wonderstruck
      Who worship God as their Guru instructs.
      Faithfully they practice what they have been taught
      These shall pass death's heavy onslaught.

26   Arjuna, realize that forms emanate
      When the Knower touches the field.
      By this touching He creates
      Yet forever transcends the yield.

27   That soul who sees the Highest Lord
      As not decaying when all else perishes,
      As dwelling equally in every being,
      That soul, indeed, is truly seeing.

28   When a soul sees the Lord everywhere,
      He offers no outrage to his own self anywhere.
      Then no longer hidden is the Vision of the Lord
      The soul sings at-one-ment with the cosmic chord.

29   That soul understands that every action
      Is of nature, that Spirit is actionless.
      Matter performs each act and every deed
      Independent of the soul's hope or creed.

30   When a soul sees the varied states
      In which the creatures radiate,
      As being That which abides in the One,
      That soul merges with the Cosmic Sun.

31   The Higher Self is beginningless
      Without process of change and endless.
      Even when in body It remains,
      It never acts, It obtains no stains.

32   Just as the ether pervading all things
      Is far too subtle to be stained,
      So the Spirit dwelling within,
      Cannot be stained by any whim.

33   Arjuna, as all is illumined by a single sun,
      One Spirit illumines the field and everyone.
      And so the Knower of the field
      Illumines the total spinning wheel.

34   Those who in Vision know the distinction
      Between the field and its Knower,
      Through the opening of the Wisdom Eye
      Advance to the Holy One on High.

The Yoga of the Three Strands

14

1   Arjuna, once again I relate to you
    This highest mystic wisdom.
    Sages through all ages have found it so:
    Earth does Heaven bestow.

2   Acquiring this Holy Ancient Wisdom,
    The sage is not born when a new age begins.
    His soul is not disturbed at dissolution time
    For he is a consciousness akin to Mine.

3   My primordial undeveloped nature
    Is the Cosmic Womb of each creature.
    Therein I place the Seed of Consciousness;
    The birth of all flows from this mingling.

4   Of whatever size or shape or form, indeed,
    I am the Father, the giving seed.
    The Great Mother Matter is the womb,
    And thus life is woven on its loom.

5   Darkness, Fire and Light
    These strands spring from Nature,
    These are the bonds that bind
    The Undying One to the body blind.

6   Of these, Light is immaculate
     Bringing Illumination immediate.
     Yet it binds the soul attached to bliss,
     Longing for knowledge and the wisdom kiss.

7   Of these, Fire is full of desire
     Thirstily eager for things to acquire.
     Such lust will bind the embodied one
     By attaching to fruits-of-action won.

8   Of these, Darkness is full of ignorance
     Deluding the embodied with indifference.
     Attaching them with heedlessness
     By means of sloth and sleepiness.

9   Light attaches a soul to wisdom,
     Darkness to obscuring gloom,
     Fire attaches a soul to action's desire;
     Each is a bond to the soul's rising higher.

10   Light can prevail over fire and darkness,
     Or fire can curtail the light and the dark
     Or darkness prevail over fire and light;
     As one prevails, it suppresses the other's might.

11   When the light of knowledge shines
     At every one of the body's gates,
     Then compassion reigns supreme
     And a soul can walk to the higher dream.

12   When the fiery guna dominates,
     Activity, restlessness, greed and pride
     Are the conditions of mind that arise,
     Awakening ambition and craving enterprise.

13   When the darkness dominates
     The following conditions fill the slate:
     Slothfulness and laziness,
     A mind deluded with heedlessness.

14   If a person passes when light is in the ascendant,
      Attained are subtle planes and joys attendant.
      Such a dissolution is hard to obtain
      A soul of light shall not taste death's pain.

15   The person dissolved at the hour of fire
      Is reborn in a body filled with desire.
      A death occurring in the dark hour
      Brings rebirth in a body lacking power.

16   Sages say the fruit of light is happiness
      The fruit of fire is distress
      The fruit of darkness is ignorance,
      Not allowing the soul to advance.

17   Knowledge is derived from light
      And from fire arises greed,
      Ignorance is born of darkness
      From the strands, oh soul, be freed.

18   The soul of light in celestial realms creates,
      The fiery soul stays in intermediate states,
      And those of darkness fall and go
      To the unconscious realms far below.

19   When the soul perceives that only these strands
      Are the causative agents in the material land,
      He knows that I stand beyond the strands
      And enters My Being in joy to expand.

20   By transcending the three qualities,
      The soul achieves immortality.
      The gunas alone cause the changes of life:
      Birth, disease, old age, all of life's strife.

21   Krishna, what marks one who transcends the tree?
      How does one behave to be free?
      And how, Oh Lord, does a soul foresee
      The way to transcend the gunas three?

22   Arjuna, that soul who feels no aversion to light
      No aversion to darkness, no fear of fire,
      In this soul these strands no longer conspire,
      The gunas are absent, he has no desire.

23   That soul who sits as the witness of all
      Knows it is the gunas that cause the fall.
      He who is not by the qualities perturbed,
      Remains firm in Godhood and undisturbed.

24   Balanced in pleasure or pain,
      Regarding earth, stone or gold as the same,
      Remaining centered whether praised or blamed,
      That soul holds to wisdom and gains the flame.

25   Balanced in honor or disgrace
      Balanced toward friend, foe or life's race;
      By renouncing the sense of doership,
      A soul transcends guna rulership.

26   That soul who transcends the qualities
      Is fit to reach the highest samadhis,
      Is intent on Me and never swerves,
      And disciplined by wisdom, truly serves.

27   I am the Majestic Lord Aortal
      Within this body—Life Immortal!
      Unchanging Life that perishes never
      I am the Truth, the Joy and the Bliss Forever!

The Yoga of the
Supreme Self

15

1   Arjuna, the everlasting Ashwattha Tree, so sages say,
     Has its roots in Heaven, its branches earthward lay.
     Its trunk is the Creator, its leaves the wisdom-song;
     Know this Tree and live to right all wrong.

2   Its branches are fed by the gunas three,
     Sense enjoyments are its tender leaves.
     Upward and downward they extend and weave;
     Its roots bind the soul by its action-shoots.

3   This tree with its firmly growing roots
     Has not origin, middle or even end;
     Its forms are difficult to comprehend,
     So in detachment must we cut and rend.

4   Seek that supreme state to which the sages go,
     And finding it, return not to this earth below.
     In the Primeval Spirit alone find the glow,
     The beginningless Being from which all beings flow.

5   Wisdom-hearted sages that changeless state know,
     Their desire neutralized, they dwell in God's Soul.
     Not proud, not deluded, but detached they attain
     The Samadhi that frees one from pleasure and pain.

6   This Infinite Being is not illumined
     By Sun nor Moon nor even Balanced Fire.
     The unreturning sages find the eternal home
     The balanced abiding place, My Throne.

7   The Spirit in the body is eternal
     Part of Myself and non-ephemeral.
     It draws unto It a mind and senses five
     It rests in matter as the queen in the hive.

8   As the wind carries perfume from flowery blooms,
     So the soul, the Lord of the bodily room,
     Carries away the mind and senses
     When the body is entombed.

9   Indwelling in hearing and sight,
     Indwelling in touch and taste,
     The sweet fragrance of earth He partakes
     As He dwells in the body of the five sense states.

10   He senses by means of the strands, you see,
     So deluded souls do not perceive
     That He leaves the body or stays thereby,
     He is only seen by the wisdom-eye.

11   Yogis earnestly disciplined in their soul
     Are firmly fixed and find the goal.
     But the impure, no matter how they strive,
     Will surely not at the goal arrive.

12   There is a splendor in the Sun
     Whose royal effulgence radiates,
     There is a splendor in the moon and fire;
     I am that Light: all things do I Illuminate.

13   And by entering into the Earth,
     All beings I maintain;
     And by becoming the nectarian moon,
     I sustain all plants with rain.

14   By becoming the flame of life
      Foods I lovingly devour.
      I dwell in the bodies of all living beings
      Co-joining the breaths with true seeing.

15   I am installed in the hearts of all and so
      From Me comes memory, wisdom and their flow.
      Through all the scriptures I alone am known;
      I have all the holy scriptures sown.

16   In this world there are two kinds of beings:
      The perishable and the imperishable, the freeing.
      The bodies of all are chained to change
      Yet the spirit within is eternally living.

17   There is a Higher Spirit,
      The Unchanging Lord who inhabits,
      The Ancient One called the Supreme Soul,
      The support of the worlds above and below.

18   I am beyond perishable matter
      And higher than imperishable soul
      I am the Eternal Cosmic Sun
      Known as the Supreme Person.

19   That soul who recognizes Me
      As the Highest Person knows everything.
      The undeluded soul comes to Me
      With all his love in purity.

20   Arjuna, in this way, has
      The Secret Teaching been imparted today.
      Assimilating this a soul becomes wisdom
      And attains the supreme satisfaction.

The Divine and
Demonic Path

16

1   Arjuna, these are the traits of the holy soul
    Born to the divine state:
    Lacking ego or conceit, without hate,
    Patient and austere, thus abating fear.

2   Pure in heart and studious of soul,
    Tranquil in mind, ever seeking life's goal,
    Gentle, yet ardent, in his search harmless,
    Detached, far-sighted, and fearless.

3   Honest, good and modest in need,
    Without fickleness, without greed,
    With generosity and forbearance,
    Clinging to the Path with endurance.

4   These are the traits of the foolish soul
    Born or fallen to the demonic state:
    Hypocritical, angry, and insolent,
    Conceited, harsh and arrogant.

5   The demonic traits tend to enslave,
    The divine traits tend to set free.
    Arjuna, you have no cause to grieve
    For you were born with divine destiny.

6   Two types of beings in this world there are:
     The divine which is holy, the demonic which scars.
     The divine traits I did explain,
     Now hear of the demonic insane.

7   Demons know not right action
     Nor what is right cessation.
     They possess not internal or external purity
     They have not appropriate conductivity.

8   They think this world displays no truth pulse,
     That it only functions through impulse.
     They say there is no Lord or higher law
     That nothing is the result of ordered cause.

9   Holding fast to their opinions blind,
     They become the enemies of all mankind.
     Demonic souls of weak intelligence
     Promote cruel deeds of violence.

10   Filled with hypocrisy, pride and arrogance
     They are deluded in their own ignorance.
     They cling with insatiable desire,
     And to demonic acts aspire.

11   Tying themselves to endless cares
     They live til death in despair.
     They seek only the sensuous delights
     Believing pleasure is the highest height.

12   Anxiety binds them with a thousand chains,
     Held by desire and obsession's pains
     They obtain wealth by unwise means
     To satiate their lusting schemes.

13   They think: these things I have gained
     And those pleasures are next to be obtained.
     I own all this wealth and will have more in time
     And that wealth will also be mine.

14   These enemies I have already slain.
      Later, I shall cause others pain.
      I am master of my life, pleasure belongs to me.
      They long to obtain success through greed.

15   Deluded, these demonic souls say:
      I shall give alms, rejoice and pray,
      For I am well-situated and wealthy;
      None can be compared to me.

16   They are caught in delusion's web
      Bewildered by interests at high ebb.
      Addicted to desires are these demonic infidels
      They are already in the foulest of hells.

17   Filled with self-importance and pride
      They offer sacrifice for show and bribe.
      Deluded by conceit and filled with avarice
      They make hypocrisy of holy sacrifice.

18   These envious souls, vicious with violence,
      Detest Me in the other's body in silence,
      And in their own, where I yet abide
      Despite their wrath, desire and pride.

19   Into this transmigrating place,
      The cruel, the hateful and the base
      Return again because of their minds
      To birth in demonic wombs that bind.

20   Born again into wombs lacking mirth,
      Deluded still from rebirth to rebirth,
      And not attempting to reach Me at all
      Down to the deepest hells they fall.

21   The triple door to anguishing hell
      Is lust, anger and greed,
      From these three become freed
      For they are destructive to your true need.

22   A soul released from this triple door
       Attains Illumination to the core
       Thereby attaining the Highest Goal:
       Union with the Supreme Cosmic Soul.

23   Those who discard the principles of wisdom
       And act according to rules of their own
       Do not attain Illumination or Happiness
       Nor do they gain the supreme loveliness.

24   Therefore, let the Gita be your guide
       On your way to the other side.
       Follow the principles of the Deified.
       Perform only those actions sanctified.

The Three Paths

17

1 Krishna, some worship with faith full to the brim
Yet act according to their own whim.
What is the nature of their faithfulness
Does it belong to Light, Fire or Darkness?

2 Arjuna, faith is of three kinds:
One that frees, one that holds and one that binds.
Souls are born of light, of darkness and fire,
Hear as I tell you of each one's desire.

3 Every soul is composed of faith whole
And surely the faith of every soul
With its own inner nature must agree
And as that faith is, so is he.

4 Souls of Light have faith in the good,
Souls of Fire in the aggressive mood,
Souls of Darkness have faith in the degenerate,
Thus do the gunas shape the temperament.

5 Souls who practice extreme austerity
Do so through ego and hypocrisy.
They go beyond what the yogic law requires
They are possessed of attachment, pride and desire.

6   He who torments the organs of the body,
      Know he also torments Me.
      By extreme austerity nothing can be solved
      Such souls are ignorant and of demonic resolve.

7   Even foods that souls enjoy
      Come in three categories,
      As do charity, sacrifice and austerity;
      Each action follows the guna theory.

8   Foods that souls of light like
      Give strength, health and delight.
      They longevity and intelligence impart,
      Are sweet, bland and warm the heart.

9   Foods bitter, burned and very hot
      Are causes of pain and a short lot.
      Foods that souls of fire devour
      Are spicy, salty, dry and sour.

10   Foods that souls of darkness desire,
      Those that they truly do admire
      Are stale, spoiled and even smelly
      Rotten, decayed and dirty.

11   Worship born of the light
      Purely springs from spiritual sight
      Souls of light seek not reward's gain
      They do each task as duty ordains.

12   Worship born of the fire
      Seeks to gain the goals of desire.
      Whatever the price, they are willing to pay
      To gratify their worldly display.

13   Worship born of the darkness
      Is not sanctioned by holiness,
      Is devoid of faith, no mantra is given,
      No tithes are offered, no food is eaten.

14   Austerity of the body consists
      Of gentleness and purity that persists.
      Homage to Sages, Teachers and Guru,
      Honoring the Devas and Swamis too.

15   Austerity of speech I have heard
      Is the study of the Sacred Word,
      Speaking gently, never causing dis-ease
      Words truthful, kindly, intending to please.

16   Austerity of the mind, equanimity,
      Brings cheerfulness and tranquility.
      The habit of meditation and self-control
      Gives purity of heart, makes a gentle soul.

17   The austerity produced by the Light of Grace
      Brings to souls the Threefold Faith.
      They who practice yoga not seeking reward
      Are self-controlled and know the Lord.

18   Austerity produced by the guna fire
      Is performed for gain, with irreverence,
      Is fickle, lacking spiritual permanence,
      And done with a hypocritical countenance.

19   The austerity produced by darkness
      Comes from delusion and ignorance.
      It weakens the body and the soul,
      Or seeks to place on another control.

20   The gift that is given from Light
      Aspires for no returning grace,
      Is given to a worthy soul
      At a proper time and place.

21   The gift that is given from fire
      Aspires for a returning grace
      It is given grudgingly or by one
      Who aims at the many rewards to come.

22   The gift given from darkness
       At the improper time and place
       Is given with contempt to an unworthy soul
       Condescendingly offered without spiritual goal.

23   Om Tat Sat is the mantra threefold
       Symbolizing absolute spiritual gold.
       In ancient times these signs were told
       By sages performing the rites of old.

24   Therefore, after chanting the sacred Om,
       Give gifts, perform worship and austerity.
       The Vedas declare that such should be
       And devoted disciples do their duty.

25   After chanting Tat and not seeking reward,
       Give gifts and do acts of sacrifice.
       Such austerities bring lasting peace
       To the soul who seeks ultimate release.

26   The Divine Sat means goodness,
       That which is enjoyed in happiness.
       It is the noble action done,
       Sat is the proper balance won.

27   In worship, alms and austerities
       Steadfastness is known as Sat.
       With such goals in mind chant Tat
       And your action will be known as Sat.

28   Whatever gift is offered without faith,
       In alms, rites, austerity or text,
       Is naught in this world and naught in the next.
       Such action is asat for the soul is vexed.

The Yoga of Liberation

18

1   What is the difference between renunciation
    On the one hand and non-attachment on the other?
    Tell me, Krishna, how each leads the soul
    To the unchanging ground where one is made whole.

2   Arjuna, when a soul gives up actions of desire,
    Renunciation is what is meant;
    When a soul abandons rewards-of-action,
    This the sages call non-attachment.

3   Some say that action must be given up as ill
    But sages say: do your duty still,
    For by worship, alms and austerity
    The human soul is filled.

4   Arjuna, it is My conclusion
    After due resolution
    That non-attachment is best understood
    As the threefold discipline in the good.

5   A soul ought not to abandon spirituality:
    Worship, alms or austerity,
    Because these three actions of self-control
    Even purify souls that are whole.

6   These actions which are to be done
    Must with non-attachment be begun.
    They should be performed with joyous mind:
    This is My supreme decree to mankind.

7   When abandonment belongs to the dark side,
    Souls digress from the duty prescribed.
    They act improperly and are bemired
    For by delusion they are inspired.

8   When abandonment belongs to fire,
    A soul longs for pleasure's desire.
    Such souls do not obtain spiritual benefit
    For their actions are counterfeit.

9   When abandonment belongs to light,
    Right action brings spiritual sight.
    Such souls know that duty's to be done
    And so are detached from the fruit that is won.

10 Moved by Light, a soul is God's handiwork
    And thus never hates unpleasant work.
    All doubts removed, the wise never shirk,
    Neither do they cling to any pleasant work.

11 While embodied, no soul can
    Abandon all work completely;
    But that soul who abandons desire for gain
    Knows renunciation and thus abstains.

12 Efforts produce results of three kinds:
    The sought, the unsought, the two combined
    Actualized after death for those attached
    But not for the souls who remain unlatched.

13 In Sankhya philosophy
    Five major causes of effort are declared
    Therefore be thou effectively prepared
    Know the cause of all action everywhere.

14   The body, the doer and the senses,
      And also actions of various kinds,
      As well as the supersoul deva of destiny
      Are the causes of all that bind.

15   Whatever action a soul undertakes
      These five forces to that action belong,
      Whether in body, speech or thought
      Whether the action be right or wrong.

16   The soul who thinks that it knows
      That the agent is the self alone
      Thinks so because the mind's undisciplined
      This soul sees not, Truth is overthrown.

17   In a soul not bound by ego,
      With Enlightenment burning bright,
      Though he destroy his world's delight
      He never slays, his soul remains white.

18   Knowledge, object and the knower
      Compose the threefold cause of action
      The senses, karma and the doer
      Are the threefold basis of activation.

19   Knowledge, effort and the doer
      In the theory of the strands
      Differ in quality and are three in kind
      Hear now how they affect the mind.

20   Knowledge that is of light
      Reveals a deathless being who unites
      In each and every creature;
      Centered wisdom merges every feature.

21   Knowledge that is of fire
      Sees difference because of nomenclature.
      Thus many souls with many features
      Seem apart from their fellow creatures.

22   Knowledge of darkness knows
       No reason, sees no light.
       It takes part of nature as the whole
       And thus misreads nature's Holy Soul.

23   Karma derived from light
       Is performed without desire or hate
       By those who know God awaits.
       They are detached, and do not hesitate.

24   Karma derived from fire
       Is intent with desire.
       It has much energy to expend
       For its own selfish ends.

25   Karma derived from darkness
       Issues from disregarding consequence.
       Because of this deluded sense
       Violence reigns with indifference.

26   The doer without desire
       Has energy and steadfastness
       Is detached and fearless,
       Is open-hearted in failure or success.

27   The doer with desires
       Enjoys, grieves and strives.
       Rewards for effort he procures
       And thus Enlightenment he obscures.

28   The doer that is indifferent
       Is undisciplined, proud and low
       He is dishonest, lazy and a detriment,
       Depressed and also slow.

29   Arjuna, now hear knowledge first-hand
       Concerning insight into the earth's lands.
       All actions are composed of the three which merge
       According to the theory of the guna's urge.

30   Insight born of light that does not cease
        Knows the difference between bondage and release,
        Between action and cessation, calmness and fear;
        Its instinct to duty comes from the Seer.

31   Insight born of fire
        Cannot discern between duty and desire
        Between what ought and ought not be done
        Between duty and things that are fun.

32   Insight born of darkness
        Thinks what's wrong is right.
        All things become opposed,
        Ignorance obscures the light.

33   Confidence derived from light is emphasized
        By constant yogic exercise,
        Bringing restraint of all activities
        Of mind, breath and the sense keys.

34   Confidence derived from fire
        Causes attachment to hold tight
        To wealth, desire or the right.
        In grasping reward, the fiery fight.

35   Confidence derived from darkness
        Causes the fool not to put aside
        His sorrow, cowardice or distress
        His dependency or pride.

36   And now at last the threefold happiness
        I shall expound, if you will attend.
        With this threefold joy a soul knows practice
        And all its sorrows come to an end.

37   The happiness espoused of the Holy Light
        Flowers in the soul who finds delight
        Transforming all things into tranquility,
        A soul of light sees only spirituality.

38   Happiness espoused of fire
       Burns when an object touches a sense;
       First it is nectar but then a poison pyre
       And in the end, brings dire consequence.

39   Happiness espoused of darkness
       Causes the soul to be led astray
       In both the beginning and the end they say
       Because of carelessness, sloth and decay.

40   There is nothing on the earth
       Or in the realm of the divinities
       That is free from that which comes
       From the three natural qualities.

41   For priests, warriors and furthermore
       For merchants and for serfs
       All have differences accounted for accurately
       By the proper inborn qualities.

42   A priest's work is gaining knowledge of the good,
       Teaching confidence and patience, sharing Sandalwood.
       In the Dharma such souls find life's Goal,
       In austerity, goodness and self-control.

43   The warrior's natural work is to protect the right
       And never to flee from the righteous fight.
       With deep abiding magnanimity
       They live in courage and majesty.

44   The merchant's natural work is trade,
       Herding and cultivation of the soil;
       Serfs have their natural work set aside
       In service to others which consists of toil.

45   Each soul achieves his own ultimate success
       By putting forth his own best effort effortless.
       Allow Me to tell you how success is won:
       Do your own duty, as seen by your Inward Sun.

46   A soul wins success by attuning to That
      From which all else has emerged,
      That in which the universe is submerged,
      And by following the Way all karmic paths converge.

47   It is wiser to do your own duty ill
      Than to do another's with skill.
      Doing the duty that to you pertains
      Produces on your soul no karmic stains.

48   No soul should stop the work allotted
      Even though weary or even plague spotted.
      Every endeavor has its own saturn
      Misleading can be the first visual pattern.

49   For a mind detached from all objects will be
      Self-conquered and from longing free.
      That soul finds through non-attachment
      A perfect inaction harmony.

50   Listen as I offer explanation:
      Having first found purity of heart, perfection,
      You may then attain the highest goal
      Complete union with God's wisdom soul.

51   Restraining the senses with spiritual consistency,
      Cleansed and endowed with a clear-seeing brilliancy
      Abandon elation and depression
      Make hearing and seeing acts of purification.

52   With body, speech and mind under control,
      Cultivate desirelessness as your life's goal.
      Always practice holy yogic meditation,
      Live in quietude and eat in moderation.

53   A soul suited for becoming enlightened
      Is beyond aggression, pride and greed
      Is lifted beyond selfishness
      From ego, anger and desire is freed.

54   Becoming illumined and calm of soul,
        You see that love for Me is the goal.
        And by neither coveting nor disagreeing
        You shall be balanced to every being.

55   By divine love you recognize Me
        And enter into Me lovingly.
        You see My holiness and become My friend
        By knowing that I dwell within.

56   Though souls put trust in Me
        They continue to give an effort great
        And through My grace, they then achieve
        The eternal and unchanging samadhi state.

57   Make Me your goal and in your thought
        Be devoted to Me and ever self-taught.
        In all your actions to Me be resigned
        And resolve to attain a disciplined mind.

58   Attune to Me, for by My grace
        All obstacles shall be erased.
        If you hold to the ego, you will be debased
        And cannot behold My holy face.

59   If impelled by your own ego, and without foresight,
        You say the words, I will not fight,
        Your resolution will be in vain
        And your holy nature be constrained.

60   Held fast by your natural constitution,
        And by the blindness of your delusion
        Whatsoever you try not to do
        You will be impelled to pursue.

61   In the heart of every being
        The Lord abides propelling.
        He causes by His Maya all to spin
        And Life to be determined from deep within.

62   Find assurance in Me alone for release
      And you will attain the highest peace.
      Love Me with all your being and by My grace
      You will find My eternal abiding place.

63   This wisdom as expounded by Me
      Is the profoundest of profundity.
      Consider it truly and ponder on it
      Then act as you consider fit.

64   The greatest truth of all, My highest word,
      I now impart, let it be understood.
      My friend, you are so beloved by Me
      My good counsel is for thee.

65   Show love to Me and bear Me in mind.
      Attune to Me and with Me intertwine.
      I promise you will be Illumined in Me
      Because you are My own destiny.

66   Discarding all other dharmas,
      Seek assurance in Me alone
      And from every ill and all trauma
      I shall free you with seeds unsown.

67   This counsel is for you, not for everyone
      For without austerity, there is no Inner Sun.
      It is not for those who live in doubt
      Who are disobedient and not devout.

68   That soul who teaches My greatest secret
      Will show the highest love for Me.
      To My own devotees this love he shows
      And thus without doubt, to Me he goes.

69   And among all mankind
      None loves Me more than he
      Nor shall there ever be on earth
      Another soul more dear to Me.

70   Whosoever will study this yoga
       Concerning super abundant light
       Will through the worship of wisdom
       Attune to Me and My fullest delight.

71   And whosoever simply listens in confidence
       And without complaints proceeds,
       Finds release in the Lord of his dreams
       And dwells with the soul of virtuous deeds.

72   Arjuna, you have attended to My words
       My thoughts you have in meditation held.
       I ask, are your ignorance
       And confusion now dispelled?

73   Krishna, my confusion is ended
       Attending to the Truth I heard.
       Through your grace my doubts are dispersed
       I stand and shall carry out your holy word.

       Sanjaya concluded:

74   Thus from Vasudeva have I heard
       These amazing wisdom words
       Spoken between the Overlord and His soul:
       Sri Krishna and Arjuna of self-control.

75   For I heard by the grace of Vyasa
       The science of Kriya from the Lord of Yoga.
       Thus Sri Krishna's highest mystery
       Was explained to me personally.

76   As I remember and as I recall
       This discourse wondrous and most sublime
       In which Sri Krishna taught the terrestrial
       I am filled with bliss each and every time.

77 And more and more I am filled with bliss
   Because of the wondrous ectogenesis
   As I remember and as I recall
   Sri Hari's most wondrous form of all.

78 Wherever Sri Krishna, the Yoga Lord may be
   Whenever Arjuna lifts his bow
   There reigns victory and glorious yoga siddhi
   This is my conviction, for this I know.

   Thus in the Upanishad, sung by the Lord,
   The science of Brahman, the Scripture of Yoga,
   The dialogue between Sri Krishna and Arjuna ends.

   Om Tat Sat Om.

Glossary

Ananta: The cosmic serpent, symbolizing creative energy, upon which Lord Vishnu rests.

Arjuna: One of the five Pandava brothers, symbolical of the earthling.

Asan: A yogic posture used to attain deep meditation and the release of spiritual energies.

Asat Karma: Difficult or obstructive karma hindering spiritual unfoldment.

Asita: The Lord of yoga siddhis (divine energies) who guards and protects.

Atma: The Self, the inner Reality of our being, the microcosm.

Aum: (See Om.)

Avatar: The incarnation of God on the earth, or the descent of divine consciousness into the heart of man; a theophany which, according to Hindu epics, appears in various ages when goodness grows weak and evil increases.

Bhisma: Commander in chief of the Kauravas.

Blind King, The: (See Dhritarashtra.)

Brahma: The principle of creation of the Hindu Trinity (Brahma, Vishnu, and Shiva).

Brahman: The Ultimate Reality, the macrocosm.

Devas: High celestial beings.

Dharma: The cosmic law which sustains and upholds all things in unity.

Dhritarashtra: The Blind King of the Kauravas clan to whom Sanjaya relates the entire battle of Kurukshtra, clairaudiently and clairvoyantly, as they sit in the palace.

Drona: Military leader of the Kuru clan.

Duryodhana: The eldest son of Dhritarashtra, leader of the Kauravas army.

Gunas: The three modes or strands which cause the evolution of matter: darkness, fire and light.

Hari: One of the names of Lord Vishnu.

Karma: The law of causation on all levels of existence.

Kauravas: The sons of the Blind King, symbols of greed, ruthlessness, and ambition.

Krishna: One of the key divine incarnations of Lord Vishnu.

Kriya: The spiritual science of balanced Self-conscious awareness.

Kurus: The clan to which Arjuna belongs.

Kusa Grass: A species of grass (commonly called darbha) used for making matting, regarded as most sacred.

Loka: A plane of existence.

Mantra: A sacred sound chanted to invoke a mystical state of consciousness.

Manu: The ancient law-giver.

Maya: The emanent aspect of transcendent reality, the form of the formless.

Mount Meru: The axis of the universe.

Naga: A serpent or elephant, symbolizing the basic creative energies.

Om: The holy word, the cosmic reverberation from which all is created. Also spelled Aum.

Om tat sat om: The mystical Tetragrammaton of balanced self-conscious awareness.

Pandavas: The sons of Pandu, Arjuna and his four brothers, the enemies of the Kauravas.

Pandu: A dynasty of Indian kings to which the Pandavas belong.

Rishi: An inspired sage.

Samadhi: Conscious trance through which cosmic consciousness manifests.

Sandalwood: Holy wood and/or holy oil that is used by priests.

Sanjaya: The sage who relates the Gita to the Blind King.

Sankhya: One of the six orthodox schools of Hindu philosophy.

Shanti: A yogic mantra which means 'Peace'.

Shiva: The Lord of redissolvement, the protector and benefactor of yogis.

Siddhi: Mystical, spiritual energies or powers.

Soma: Mystical, astral energy that involves visual states.

Sri: A title of respect originally meaning holy or honored.

Strands: (See gunas.)

Swami: A Hindu or a yogic priest.

Upanishads: The mystical texts found at the end of the Vedas, the direct revelation of Truth by the sages.

Vasudeva: A name of Lord Krishna and the father of Lord Krishna. In yogic terms, Lord of the sustaining life-breath.

Vedas: The primary Hindu scriptures.

Vishnu: The Lord of preservation who incarnates from age to age to re-establish the Dharma.

Vyasa: Compiler of the Vedas.

Yoga: The path, disciplines, and techniques which lead to cosmic consciousness.

Notes

Excerpts from other books by Goswami Kriyananda you
may enjoy:

A Beginner's Guide to Meditation
Meditation is the art of inturning, focusing, and
balancing the forces of your mind to a point of peace and
tranquility. In the calmness of the meditative mind, all
polarities are harmonized into a stillness, which is
eternal, unchanging, and ever blissful.

There is a place deep within you, where you can go to find
peace, life-direction, and, indeed, the supreme happiness.

The Intermediate Guide to Meditation
Meditation is a way of clearly seeing what you need in this
life, and why. To formally meditate is to learn to truly see
the law of life. The law of life is what is generated through
you. And while it radiates out from you, it always radiates
stronger within you. Thus, my guru once remarked,
'That which one does unto another soul, one does more
so unto his own self.' I feel, however, that which a soul
tries to do unto another, he does more so unto himself.

Intermediate meditation is the application of meditation
to solving everyday life problems. As stated, meditation is
a way to liberate yourself from the limitations of your own
mind. It is training the mind to move away from limited
conceptualized thinking and damaging emotionality to
expansive, non-conceptualized mind processes.

The Wisdom and Way of Astrology
Is astrology a science or is astrology a spiritual art?
Astrology, properly understood, is both a science and a
spiritual art. It is scientific in its mathematical calcula-
tions, in its consistency of interpretation, and in its direct
correlation with the heavenly bodies. It is a spiritual art in
that it explains the paradoxes of existence and reveals the
plan of life, thus, the life-plan of individuals. Astrology as

a spiritual art gives great inspiration and understanding
as to the 'why' of pain and suffering.

The meaning of astrology is to gain wisdom so that we
might find a way to live that is insightful. Wisdom allows
us to see which actions are astute. There is a moment of
maturity in which the soul transcends the bondage of
'fear' and 'apprehension,' seeking trustworthiness. Thus
he realizes the Truth has set him free.

Of all sciences, astrology is the most spiritual for it insists
that you can know the meaning, the nature, and even the
purpose of life; you do not have to depend upon another
person.

Extraordinary Spiritual Potential
The techniques utilized in this text will aid in increasing
your intuition. ESP and intuition have a great deal to do
with psychic development. Psychic development is based
upon various occult techniques that allow you to focus
your mind, attune it, and at the same time release the
balanced energies from the subconscious mind. These
balanced energies are called intuitional forces.

I always like to ask business executives and successful
people to what they attribute their extraordinary success.
Without fail, every one of them has said, "It is because of
my intuition. After I get done with all my logical thinking
and analyze all my data, I sit down and simply feel what
needs to be done next. Sometimes this goes against my
logic and data, but I follow it.

The Spiritual Science of Kriya Yoga
Kriya Yoga is the art of total balance, the science of
harmonizing the disparate parts of the being into
wholeness, a way of creative living. *The Spiritual Science of
Kriya Yoga* is a handbook and a map for your journey to
completeness.

The purpose of this text is to assist you in searching out the inner way. The inner way is the release from externalized values that have only mechanized and brutalized man's mind, causing him to destroy that which is beautiful and meaningful. This text is a spiritual map for the conquest of the inner life and the exploration of the cosmic universe that dwells within. Some of the more closely guarded secrets or techniques that will help you to walk the pathway are given. This, therefore, is a manual for mystics.

Additional materials:

Audio and video tapes covering topics such as meditation, the yogic laws of karma, astral projection and the chakras are available from The Temple of Kriya Yoga. A free catalogue of all of Goswami Kriyananda's books and audio/video tapes is available upon request.

The Temple of Kriya Yoga
2414 N. Kedzie Blvd., Dept. BG
Chicago, IL 60647
Illinois residents: (312) 342-4600
Phone orders outside Illinois: 1(800) 248-0024

(See final page for order form)

119

Order Form

Title	Quantity	Price
_____	_____	_____
_____	_____	_____
_____	_____	_____
_____	_____	_____

Shipping: $3.00

Total $ _____

☐ Yes, please send me a free catalogue of Goswami
Kriyananda's books, and audio/video tapes.

Name _____

Address _____

City _____ State _____ Zip _____

Phone: (h) _____ (w) _____

Enclosed is $ _____

☐ Check
☐ Money order
☐ Visa
☐ MasterCard

Card # _____ Exp. date _____

Signature _____

Mail orders to:
The Temple of Kriya Yoga
2414 N. Kedzie, Dept. BG
Chicago, IL 60647
(312) 342-4600

Phone orders outside Illinois: 1(800) 248-0024